POLITICS IN SOUTH AFRICA

FROM VORSTER
TO DE KLERK

Other titles in this series

Politics in Britain: From Callaghan to Thatcher (new edition)
Politics in China: From Mao to the post-Deng era (new edition)
Politics in France: From Giscard to Mitterrand (new edition)
Politics in the Soviet Union: From Brezhnev to Gorbachev
Politics in the United States: From Carter to Bush (new edition)
Politics in Germany: From Division to Unification (new edition)
World Political Systems: An Introduction to Comparative
　　Government

About the series

Chambers Political Spotlights aim to provide a bridge between
conventional textbooks and contemporary reporting. Each
title examines the key political, economic and social changes of
the country, providing, in addition, a brief contextual
background to each development discussed.

Politics in South Africa

Keith Maguire is Senior Lecturer in the School of Public
Administration and Law at Robert Gordon's Institute of
Technology, Aberdeen. A number of his articles have
appeared in academic journals.

POLITICS IN SOUTH AFRICA

FROM VORSTER TO DE KLERK

Keith Maguire

General Editor
Ian Derbyshire

Chambers

Published 1991 by W & R Chambers Ltd,
43–45 Annandale Street, Edinburgh EH7 4AZ

British Library Cataloguing in Publication Data

A catalogue record for this book is available from the British
Library.

ISBN 0-550-20752-X

Acknowledgments

I owe enormous thanks to Alastair Fyfe Holmes of W & R Chambers
Ltd for his help and patience on this project and also to my
colleague Dr Alistair McCulloch of the School of Public
Administration and Law, RGIT. Finally, I would like to thank
Anita and Eleanor for their support, and endurance, while I was
absent at the word-processor. I dedicate this book to my parents.

Cover design by James Hutcheson

Typeset by Buccleuch Printers Ltd, Hawick
Printed in England by Clays Ltd, St Ives, plc

Preface

This book continues the series of *Chambers Political Spotlights* and moves to the controversial subject of South Africa. This series of books was conceived as bridging the gap between conventional academic textbooks and contemporary events, and of providing students, teachers and the general reader with a guide through the political and social developments during recent years.

Important political, economic and social changes have been considered as objectively as possible and the historical narrative has been supported with both maps and the relevant statistical material.

Events in South Africa have undergone rapid, profound and dramatic changes in the last few years and no account of events will ever be completely up-to-date. However, an attempt to analyze and summarize these developments remains a worthwhile and important task.

Contents

Introduction   1

Chapter 1   South Africa: 1910–78   5
             South Africa: Background   5
             South Africa in Comparative Perspective   6
             The Afrikaner Opposition   13
             Afrikaner Nationalism in Power   16

Chapter 2   The Rise of P. W. Botha   25
             The Information Scandal   25
             Botha in Charge   27
             The Conservative Opposition   30
             Other White Opposition   34
             Botha's Achievements   36
             De Klerk and Reform   37

Chapter 3   Foreign and Defence Policy   39
             South African Intervention in Angola   43
             The Fall of Rhodesia   47
             Total Onslaught   50
             Nkomati and After   52
             The South African Security Apparatus   57
             The SADF in Comparative Perspective   67
             Towards a Regional Peace?   69

Chapter 4   Social and Economic Developments   71
             The South African Economy   71
             Recent Economic Trends   71
             Recent Demographic Trends   73
             The Black, Asian and Coloured Population   75
             The Mining Sector   77
             The Manufacturing Sector   85
             The Agricultural Sector   89
             The Sanctions Debate   90
             The Interests of White Labour   98
             The Black Workers   100

Chapter 5   The Internal Opposition   104
              From Defiance to Rivonia   107
              Sobukwe and the PAC   111
              The ANC: From Morogoro to Kabwe   114
              Steve Biko and Black Consciousness   118
              Buthelezi and Inkatha   120
              The Churches, the UDF and COSATU   124
              Prospects for a Solution   128

Appendix A   Prime Ministers and State Presidents: 1910–91   133
Appendix B   Public Administration in South Africa under
                 P. W. Botha   134
Appendix C   The Media in South Africa   137

Abbreviations and Glossary of Political Terms   140
Bibliography   143
Chronology of Recent Events: 1976–91   146
Index   149

Introduction

The South African question has been almost continually in the news since 1976. The country's system of government based on a racially restricted franchise has made modern South Africa something of a pariah state in the international community. Yet only a few decades ago there were similar white minority governments in other parts of Africa and even in a number of the southern states of the United States of America.

The South African issue also raises a number of difficult questions for the people of Great Britain. The political and moral values of the British people could no longer support a system of government based on racial discrimination along the South African model. Yet several decades ago, British politicians would have found no difficulty in sympathizing with the values and attitudes that remain so predominant among South African whites today.

Britain has given up its empire and has itself become a multiracial society. The British people and all the major political parties are committed to a multiracial Britain and only the neo-Nazi fringe groups talk of Britain as a white country with a non-white immigrant problem. Yet as the selection of a black Conservative parliamentary candidate in Cheltenham, in 1991, has shown, there is still a strong undercurrent of anti-black prejudice on the part of sections of the white population.

Despite the bitterness of the Boer War, Britain has maintained cordial relations with the white rulers of South Africa, particularly during the Smuts era but even with the Nationalists from Malan to Vorster. Yet during the 1970s Britain made significant moves towards integrating its non-European population by strengthening its anti-discrimination laws and practices. Furthermore, values changed among the white British towards the non-European population and once these values had changed, it was impossible to reconcile accepting discrimination abroad while condemning it at home. While Britain was changing, a small number of white British, who did not endorse these changes, emigrated to Rhodesia and South Africa where they found the climate of race relations more to their taste.

There remains a very large number of white South Africans who are entitled to residence in Britain, should they so desire it. This makes British relations with South Africa difficult because there are so many British whites who have kith and kin connections with South Africa, that the government cannot afford to ignore their wishes. At the same time many British companies have substantial investments in South Africa and although they have criticized apartheid, they have not wished unduly to antagonize Nationalist governments there. On the other hand, Britain's black population can hardly be expected to endorse approval of apartheid and since the majority of countries belonging to the British Commonwealth have ceased to be white, Britain has come under considerable pressure from this forum to take a more active role in opposing apartheid.

British politicians of most parties could sympathize with the white liberal opposition during the 1960s and 1970s but many on the right could not endorse the two major opposition groups, the African National Congress (ANC), and the Pan-Africanist Congress (PAC). The ANC was viewed with suspicion because of the powerful influence of the South African Communist Party in its upper echelons, its close ties with the Soviet Union, the Marxist rhetoric of its statements and its endorsement of the armed struggle, while the PAC seemed to substitute black prejudices for white ones.

Although after 1979 those on the British left found no difficulty in coming to terms with the ANC, those in the centre and the right of British politics have faced a series of dilemmas on South Africa. Should they oppose apartheid and risk alienating a substantial section of the white population and face possible large-scale white immigration from South Africa with all the implications that that might have for a multiracial society? What might the risks be for British business and security interests in South Africa should the Nationalists be alienated but not ousted? Or, if they were ousted, what might the implications be in terms of geopolitics should a pro-Soviet party come to power? Yet failure to condemn apartheid would be seen as sympathizing, if not actually supporting it, by both the black community in Britain and the international community including both the European Community and the Commonwealth.

During the 1980s Britain wished to see some form of substantial reform that offered a real share of political power to South African blacks. President Botha, for a variety of reasons, was unable and unwilling to deliver on this issue. To this end, British leaders consistently called for the release of Nelson Mandela and for negotiations between the National Party and the black opposition. The ANC, for its part, continued to engage in guerrilla warfare and to develop closer links with the Soviet Union. Some British politicians feared that the ANC's war would become a racial war as had almost happened in Rhodesia. During that conflict white public opinion in Britain had been very sensitive to the atrocities carried out against white civilians (many of whom were British citizens or of British descent) by the black Zimbabwean guerrilla forces.

British policy towards South Africa during the 1980s was reduced to hoping that eventually the whites would see sense and negotiate with the blacks and that the major black groups would become less pro-Marxist and that both sides could agree to a multiracial capitalist democracy. Britain did not want to see South Africa become another one-party authoritarian dictatorship like those that sadly characterized so many African states.

This book is aimed at bridging the gap between the teacher, the student and the general reader. Students who wish to look in more detail at the subject should consult the works by Davenport, Lipton, Pottinger, Giliomee and Schlemmer that are cited in the bibliography.

Keith Maguire

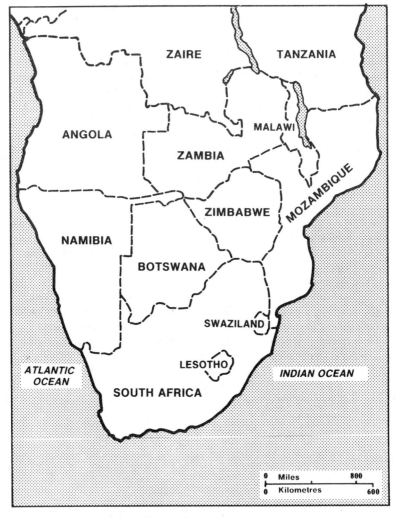

Figure 1   Southern Africa

Chapter 1

SOUTH AFRICA: 1910–78

South Africa: Background

South Africa is a country of many contrasts. It is unique for many reasons, not least its form of government based on the exclusion of its black population from any share of political power. South Africa covers a variation in terms of climate and topography. Its land surface covers 472 000 square miles. Its major rivers are the Orange and the Vaal. South Africa is divided into four provinces and a series of black homelands, which have varying degrees of self-government. The provinces are: Cape Province, Natal, the Transvaal and the Orange Free State. The state capital of South Africa is Pretoria in the Transvaal, although the parliament is situated in Cape Town in the Cape Province. The judicial capital of South Africa is Bloemfontein in the Orange Free State. The homelands are Transkei, Ciskei, Venda, Bophuthatswana, Lebowa, QwaQwa, KwaZulu, Gazankulu and Kangwane.

The reason for the decentralization of the functions of government was to be found in South Africa's history. Cape Town had always been the capital of British South Africa, while Pretoria and Bloemfontein were the capitals of the Boer states, the Transvaal and the Orange Free State. Between the aftermath of the Boer War and the formation of the Union of South Africa in 1910, part of the attempt to heal the wounds between the British and the Afrikaners was the division of the functions of state between the capitals of the different provinces. The object of this exercise was to ensure that neither side was behaving in a triumphalist fashion over the other.

The Treaty of Union in 1910 joined together the four provinces of South Africa in one political unit. South Africa was then governed under dominion status until 1961. South Africa elected its own Prime Minister but retained a governor-general and retained the British monarch as the official head of state. In 1961 the National Party, under the leadership of Dr H.F. Verwoerd, declared a republic and left the British Commonwealth.

South Africa in Comparative Perspective

South Africa is the economic giant of the African continent. The citizens of South Africa have the highest per capita income of any state in sub-Saharan Africa. The following two tables illustrate the differences between, first, South Africa and the other frontline states and, second, with a sample of some of the other important countries in Africa, including some countries which are Marxist one-party states, others that are pro-Western and others that are in a transitional stage of development.

POPULATION AND PER CAPITA INCOME: SOUTH AFRICA AND OTHER AFRICAN STATES

Country	Population (in millions)	Per Capita Income (in US dollars)
South Africa	39.0	2,300
Angola	8.6	534
Botswana	1.2	1,100
Malawi	9.1	160
Mozambique	14.6	100
Tanzania	26.0	160
Zambia	8.1	290
Zimbabwe	10.1	660
Ethiopia	52.0	120
Ghana	15.0	400
Kenya	25.0	360
Nigeria	119.0	290
Rwanda	7.6	310
Senegal	7.7	630

It is clear from these figures that the income of South Africans is far higher than that of any of her neighbours. It is also obvious that the economic performance of the states governed by Marxist regimes (Angola, Ethiopia and Mozambique) is catastrophic and partly explains the fear of a Marxist takeover in South Africa among sections of both the white population and the Inkatha Freedom Party. Where Marxist groups came to power, their rule led to the swift decline in economic performance, as was particularly the case in Mozambique. Furthermore in Angola, Ethiopia and Mozambique, the Marxist groups tended to be recruited from one ethnic group and, once in power, they swiftly began the repression of other ethnic groups.

There are other indicators that provide a revealing insight into living standards, such as life expectancy and infant mortality. Once again, South Africa has better figures than most of her neighbours and the vast majority of other countries on the continent.

**LIFE EXPECTANCY AND INFANT MORTALITY RATES:
SOUTH AFRICA AND OTHER AFRICAN STATES**

Country	Life Expectancy (in years)	Infant Mortality (per 1,000 live births)
South Africa	61	52
Angola	45	158
Botswana	67	43
Malawi	47	130
Mozambique	48	138
Tanzania	53	107
Zambia	53	80
Zimbabwe	63	65
Ethiopia	47	116
Ghana	54	89
Kenya	59	60
Nigeria	51	119

The effects of prolonged drought, famine, civil war and most recently the AIDS (Acquired Immune Deficiency Syndrome) problem are likely to further distance South Africa from her neighbours in terms of living standards. South Africa also rates well on levels of literacy and urbanization compared to most of her northern neighbours.

Yet for all of its economic advantages, South Africa is almost unique in the post-1945 era in having a democracy for its white citizens, subsequently extended to its coloured and Asian population, while effectively disenfranchising its black citizens by one means or another. This policy has earned South Africa international opprobrium and among other penalties has cost South Africa her voting rights at the United Nations.

The South African conflict has long and complicated historical roots and, even with the best of intentions from the major participants, may yet prove one of the most intractable problems of the 1990s. Judged by the standards of Western Europe and North America, the South African system of government since 1948 has seemed to be an unpleasant leftover of racial prejudice from a bygone era. Yet similar racialist outlooks were to be found in parts of the United States until the 1960s.

South Africa's system of government is unique in the respect of a white minority ruling over a majority of citizens who are not white. It is not unusual in Africa for an ethnic minority to form a government and rule a state, the majority of whose citizens belong to a different ethnic group. Furthermore, it is not unusual for them to do so without a democratic mandate. Over 80 per cent of African states are one-party or military states, where any form of political opposition is outlawed. Whereas a number of newly industrializing countries, such as Singapore, Malaysia and Taiwan, have made great economic progress since the 1960s, the same has not been true of the African continent.

South Africa alone accounts for some 34 per cent of the gross domestic product of the sub-Saharan region. Its private sector has extensive investments around the world and with it the power to compete on equal terms with American, European and Japanese competitors. South Africa, for demographic, geographic and economic reasons, has and will continue to have substantial influence on its neighbours. This makes the South African conflict and the attempt to resolve it not only a South African matter but also a southern African affair.

Since the first settlement of Europeans on the Cape of Good Hope in 1652, southern Africa has witnessed not only a conflict between the white settlers and the African tribes but also between the different settler groups. This culminated in the Anglo-Boer Wars between the British and the Dutch- and Afrikaans-speaking Boers (farmers) that ended in 1902 with the Treaty of Vereeniging.

The attempts by the culturally distinct Boers to establish their own republics in the Transvaal and the Orange Free

State were ended by the military defeats of the Boer War. Despite their numerical inferiority against the British empire, the Boers had fought hard to preserve their independence. When it had become clear that conventional tactics had failed, the Boers resorted to guerrilla strategy against the British forces. The British replied by interning Boer women and children in concentration camps and dealing out summary executions to any Boer guerrillas they captured. Just under 28 000 Boers died in the British concentration camps, with over 70 per cent of the deaths being of those under the age of sixteen.

Yet the end of the Anglo-Boer War also saw the beginning of a reconciliation between the two white communities. The British administration in the southern African colonies, under Lord Alfred Milner, hoped that the two white communities would unite under British leadership. Several of the most prominent leaders of the Boer army, such as General Jan Smuts and General Louis Botha subsequently became Prime Ministers of the country and good friends of the British empire.

The British government's policy of reconciliation towards the Boers led to the four provinces of the Cape, Natal, the Transvaal and the Orange Free State joining together to become the self-governing Union of South Africa in 1910. In what was a common feature of imperial power guilt, the British attempted to make amends for the wrongs done to one group (the Boers) by giving them something at the expense of others, namely the blacks. When the British handed over power to the House of Assembly (South Africa's parliament), they also agreed to leave the question of giving the vote to blacks for the Boers to decide. This was to leave South Africa's black majority disenfranchised for over eighty years.

Despite an initial economic dislocation, the Boers began to reassert themselves. They underwent something of a cultural renaissance in the decades following the Treaty of Vereeniging. In the first place, they endeavoured to ensure that they did not become anglicized as Milner and others had hoped. The two main pillars of their cultural separatism were their separate Afrikaans language and their Calvinist religion.

Botha led the South Africa Party to victory in the 1910 election and reconciliation between the two white communities remained his major priority. To this end, Louis Botha ensured that his cabinet included people from most sections of the white community. Not all the Boers believed that white unity was the most important political goal: some, for example Barry Hertzog, personified the latent anglophobia within the Boer community. Hertzog argued that the preservation of the Boer identity was of paramount significance and that Anglicization and British imperialism were the greatest threats to the Boer community.

Hertzog attacked Botha's policy of South Africa participating in the First World War on the British side, remembering the sympathy that the German Kaiser had shown to the Boer cause in the past. A number of former Boer commandos attempted a rising against the war effort but were suppressed by government troops. Smuts, however, wholeheartedly supported the British war effort, believing that a victory over the Germans would extend South African influence not only into South-West Africa but also into East Africa. South African forces fought for the allies in Africa and also participated on the Western Front, where they suffered extremely high casualties.

In 1919 Jan Smuts became Prime Minister following the sudden death of Louis Botha. As Smuts had hoped, the allied victory gave the South African government a mandate from the League of Nations to administer the former German colony of South-West Africa but the South Africans were not successful in their attempt to take over the various British territories along their borders.

The fruits of war were not to last long for Smuts. Before 1914 the South African government had faced growing opposition from organized white labour in the goldfields and this opposition was to become more militant in the aftermath of the war. After 1920 the mine-owners attempted to reduce their costs by reversing their policies of reserving skilled jobs for whites only. The white miners went on strike against the loss of their privileges. Although initially Smuts had tried to be conciliatory, ultimately he came down on the side of the mine-owners, who were mainly of British rather than Boer descent.

Smuts suppressed the strike with great force, an action that contributed to his unpopularity with working-class Afrikaners. Hertzog, the leader of the National Party, and Cresswell, the leader of the Labour Party, decided to form a pact for the next general election in order to oust Smuts and the South Africa

Party from government. The National Party had promised its leftist allies that it would not alter relationships with Britain and that it would protect white workers against competition from blacks. When the next election was called in 1924, the National Party and its allies won and Hertzog became the new Prime Minister.

Hertzog's government enacted new legislation such as the 1925 Wages Act and the Mines and Works Amendment Act of 1926 that was to benefit white workers at the expense of blacks. He also introduced extensions to the public order laws in order to restrict the rights of the blacks. In foreign affairs, Hertzog moved South Africa to dominion status and set up a network of diplomatic and trading missions.

In 1929 Hertzog faced the electorate again with his leftist allies. The National Party and the South Africa Party both gained seats but the Labour Party lost support and began to disintegrate. The coloured, Asian and African communities realized that, despite the occasional flirtation, the Nationalists were not their friends. The Nationalists, too, realized that the black opposition lacked the leadership, resources, organization and external support necessary to oppose the measures of racial discrimination.

The South African government was faced with a currency that was overvalued and so made South African exports too expensive on the world market. As South Africa found it more difficult to compete in the international markets, so there were more calls for drastic measures to try to improve the country's economic position. The government considered a range of measures, including devaluation of the currency and going off the gold standard. Such measures, however, required bi-partisan support to ensure political stability and in early 1933 the National Party (under Hertzog) and the South Africa Party (under Smuts) therefore formed a coalition government. This government then embarked on a programme of retrenchment in order to combat the economic crisis and, in 1934, the two parties merged as the United South African Nationalist Party.

The United government was divided on a number of issues connected with race relations. These divisions were concerned with how the blacks and coloureds were to be electorally represented and with the laws governing the mobility and economic rights of the Africans. Those in the Smuts wing of the United Party, such as Jan Hofmeyr, tended to be more

11

liberal on matters of race relations than the Hertzogites. However, this did not prevent them from implementing legislation that was discriminatory against blacks.

In part this was because they shared certain assumptions about the role of blacks in society, but also because they regarded the unity of the fused party as being so essential that they were unwilling to provoke a confrontation with the Hertzogites. The most significant pieces of legislation under the United government were the Native Trust and Land Act (1936) and the Native Laws Amendment Act (1937) which curbed the movements and both the political and economic rights of blacks.

Ironically, it was in the area of foreign policy that the United Party faced its greatest test. The two issues that were to cause problems were the South African flag and the question of neutrality in the event of a European war. Smuts was convinced that, although South Africa had a moral right to neutrality for political and strategic reasons, involvement on Britain's side was essential in any future conflict. Hertzog did not share this view, neither did the Afrikaner Nationalist opposition.

The conflict of opinion within the United Party grew more intense with the rise of fascism in the mid-1930s. Although the United Party strongly endorsed sanctions against Mussolini's Italy for the latter's invasion of Abyssinia, the failure of the Western powers to prevent this aggression led the South Africans to be more cautious in their dealings with Nazi Germany.

Such caution was also required for other reasons. The South Africans did not want South-West Africa returned to Nazi Germany because of the security threat that this would pose. There was a large German population in South-West Africa who might legitimately have demanded incorporation into the Third Reich. In addition, many members of the Nationalist opposition, such as Verwoerd, had studied in Germany and were sympathetic to it. To antagonize these people would have led to major internal strife similar to that which occurred at the outbreak of the First World War. It was also by no means clear to what extent there was support for the Germans among the Afrikaner community.

The South African entry into the Second World War was to bring about Hertzog's downfall. As the European crisis escalated in 1939, Hertzog intended the government's policy to be one of neutrality and accordingly he introduced a motion to the House of Assembly to confirm this policy. However, Smuts spoke against neutrality and in favour of opposition to Nazi Germany and the majority in the House of Assembly supported him. One of the reasons for this was the intensely pro-Nazi apologia made by D.F. Malan and the Nationalist opposition. Hertzog then asked Sir Patrick Duncan (the governor-general) for a dissolution of the House of Assembly in order to call a general election. Sir Patrick Duncan refused and asked Jan Smuts to form a government. Smuts did so and South Africa entered the war on the allied side.

The Afrikaner Opposition

One of the most significant developments in South African politics in the interwar years was the rise of Afrikaner nationalism. A number of National Party members had been unhappy about the fusion of the South Africa Party and the National Party and they left to form the Geswuiwerde Nasionale Party (Purified National Party) in 1934.

Afrikaner nationalism had a number of distinct but inter-related strands. It comprised secular nationalism, cultural separateness from all things English but it was held together by a mixture of Calvinist teachings that emphasized the links between the Church and the community. The mobilizers of Afrikaner nationalism were urban intellectuals, teachers, dominees (clergy) and lawyers and they preached their creed to the poor Afrikaners by appealing to the values and prejudices of the countryside, the village and the Church. There was a strong element of anti-capitalism in their nationalism; after all, most of the mines and big business were the preserve of the English and the Jews. The Afrikaners were primarily a rural people, who were forced to migrate to the towns following their military defeat in the Anglo-Boer War or through economic and natural disaster, and consequently they had the traditional rural prejudices against urban dwellers.

In the cultural arena, the Broederbond set up the Federation of Afrikaans Cultural Organizations (Federasie van Afrikaanse Kultuurverenigings, FAK), which promoted the Afrikaans language and other cultural and historical events. It was in the area of historical events that the Nationalists were able to profit in the 1930s. The circumstance was the centenary of the Great Trek of 1836 when the Boers trekked from the Cape north-eastwards to Natal and the Transvaal to escape what they considered to be British discrimination against them. The Nationalists had control of the ceremonies and Henning Klopper, one of the founder members of the Broederbond, conceived the idea of re-creating the Great Trek. The centenary was a great success but it did rekindle a lot of anglophobia among the Afrikaner community, a factor which was to help the cause of the Nationalists.

The Nationalist opposition under D. F. Malan were by no means the most militant white opponents of the United Party government. South Africa had its own fascist party, the Ossewa Brandweg (Ox-Wagon Guard), led by van Rensburg. This organization was paramilitary in character and avowedly pro-Nazi. Among its members were B. J. Vorster, the future Nationalist Prime Minister and H. J. van den Bergh, the future head of the Bureau of State Security. A number of members of the Ossewa Brandweg, including Vorster and van den Bergh, were interned during the 1939–45 war.

The new Nationalists also resented the fact that they were poor and faced competition from the blacks for the low-paid and unskilled work. Those who came from the farms lacked the experience and qualifications required for skilled work. Hence the Nationalists attracted a large group of people, already discontented and ready for mobilization. Afrikaners particularly resented having to learn English, which was the language of the towns and of commerce. The new Nationalist intelligentsia formed a wide range of organizations to promote Afrikaner culture and separateness. The most powerful of these groups was the Broederbond (band of brothers). This secretive organization aimed to establish Afrikaner control of the top posts in government, the civil service, the military and business.

The Broederbond (originally known as Young South Africa) grew in power as the National Party advanced into government. They also established mutual aid societies, insurance and banking facilities to help build up a base of Afrikaner-controlled businesses. This culminated in 1942 with the creation of the Afrikaans Handelsinstituut, the Afrikaans Chamber of Commerce. Malan and his allies argued that the Afrikaners had to build up their economic as well as their political power. The Afrikaner banks, insurance companies and credit unions lent money to help establish more businesses and they also expanded into publishing and newspapers. A number of these newspapers, such as *Die Transvaaler* under the editorship of H. F. Verwoerd, were to become vocal supporters of the Nationalist cause. Smuts faced the prospect of war with concern. He had been informed that the armed forces were in a poor state of combat readiness. His initial task was to form a government, and Smuts selected a number of people from the Labour and Dominion Parties, such as W. B. Madeley and C. F. Stallard, in order to give his cabinet a broader base.

Although a substantial number of Nationalist Afrikaners opposed participation in the war, the Nationalist opposition remained bitterly divided over both policies and personality clashes between their respective leaders. Malan of the National Party did not get on with van Rensburg of the Ossewa Brandweg and neither got on with Hertzog. Smuts delegated much of domestic policy so as to concentrate on the conduct of the war. Emergency measures were used against aliens and suspected fifth columnists, while restrictions were also placed on the rights of organized labour and black labour. As in the 1914–18 war, black and coloured servicemen were assigned non-combatant roles in the armed services.

The South African forces participated in the North African and Italian campaigns during the Second World War. However, one source of conflict within South Africa was that those who volunteered to fight overseas were entitled to wear a red flash insignia, while those who remained in South Africa were not. A number of serious clashes followed between nationalist civilians and soldiers home on leave.

However, on the international scene, Smuts was to grow in stature. As the war progressed, it became clear that the Axis forces had overextended themselves and were unable to defeat both the Soviet Union and the United States. In the Far East, the dropping of the atomic bombs on Hiroshima and Nagasaki brought Japanese resistance to a sudden end. Once again Jan Smuts was to participate in the founding of an international organization, the United Nations, which it was hoped would maintain world peace.

Yet in South Africa the Smuts government lost a series of by-elections to Malan's Nationalist opposition and in 1948 the United Party coalition lost the general election to the National

Party and its allies. There were a number of reasons for this Nationalist victory. First, the Nationalists had moderated their demands for a republic, thus preserving membership of the British Commonwealth. Second, the Nationalist Party organization was much more dynamic than that of their opponents. Third, the Nationalist opposition made a number of agreements so as not to divide the anti-government vote.

There were other structural factors which aided the Nationalists, for example rural constituencies (which were more likely to be anti-government) were smaller than urban ones, thus meaning that the Nationalists required fewer votes to secure the election of a candidate. The Afrikaners traditionally had a higher birth rate than the English-speakers and so were increasing their proportion of the electorate. Some Afrikaner workers also moved to the opposition in protest against the economic advances made by blacks during the war years. They saw the black workers as rivals and so wanted their influx to the towns restricted. The Nationalists offered just such a policy, while there was suspicion that the United Party was becoming more sympathetic to blacks and less interested in white workers. There was intense suspicion of Jan Hofmeyr, who was widely seen as the heir-apparent to Smuts. Hofmeyr was perceived by many whites as being too liberal in his ideas on race relations. Other working-class Afrikaners had memories of how Smuts had crushed white labour unrest in the mines on the Rand in 1922 and hence they were keen to see his removal from office.

A further development that was likely to help the Nationalists was the growth in industrial and political protest by the black opposition. This contributed to white fears of economic and political competition and led to more sympathy for Malan and the Nationalists.

Afrikaner Nationalism in Power

In 1945 the defeat of Nazi Germany was also a defeat for doctrines of racial superiority. In the United States, more and more cases were brought before the courts challenging the laws of racial segregation in the United States Deep South. In South Africa, 1948 saw the election of a government whose entire programme amounted to an attempt to introduce policies of racial discrimination into every sphere of society.

The programme of Dr Malan and the National Party was known as apartheid (separate development). Apartheid was a political credo that drew on strong religious and biblical justifications. The arguments used to support apartheid were essentially interpretations of the Old Testament, especially the books of Genesis and Deuteronomy. The advocates of apartheid argued that all races were created separately by God and that they should not be mixed. This was interpreted to mean that interracial marriages and interracial sexual relationships were violations of God's law as stated in the Bible. Other passages of the Bible were interpreted to mean not only that different races should be kept separate but that the blacks were inferior to whites.

Support for laws restricting the freedom of the individual to choose sexual and marital partners is usually strongest among the lower echelons of the dominant ethnic group. Just as job discrimination gave the poor whites privileges in the labour market over blacks, so apartheid legislation was also to remove black, coloured and Asian males from sexual competition with poor whites. The Prohibition of Mixed Marriages Act (1949) outlawed marriages between whites and members of other racial groups. This was followed in 1950 with the Immorality Amendment Act, which made all sexual relations between whites and other racial groups illegal. However, if the races were to be kept separate, then it was necessary to ensure that all persons were allocated to one racial group. The Population Registration Act (1950) made it compulsory for everyone to be registered as a member of a racial group.

Apartheid also tried to remove the blacks from the urban areas on a permanent basis except for those who were to remain as servants of the whites. This was done with the Group Areas Act (1950), in which all racial groups were assigned separate residential areas. The Group Areas Act and the Resettlement of Natives Act (1954) also gave the government the authority to remove non-whites from areas designated as white and to transfer them to other areas. The principle of separate areas for each group might have had some degree of fairness if each group had been given land of equal quality or if each group received a proportion of land corresponding to their percentage of the population. However, the reality was that the whites took the best land and a much greater share of it than they would have been entitled to under an equitable distribution. Substantial numbers of National Party members benefited from the policy financially, too, making large profits in land speculation following the removal of non-whites from areas designated white by the National Party government.

Both liberal whites and the black opposition opposed the introduction of the National Party's policies of apartheid and launched the defiance campaign of non-violent resistance against it. The National Party in turn introduced even more draconian public order laws to contain opposition and to make organizing protests more difficult than ever for the blacks.

The National Party initially argued that its native policy was only an extension of the previous segregation policies of the Hertzog and Smuts governments. However, things were to change drastically with the appointment of Dr H. F. Verwoerd as Minister for Native Affairs in 1950. Verwoerd wanted total separation of the races with the black population removed from all the white areas. The question for Verwoerd and his supporters was what was to be done with the blacks? Apartheid legislation made it harder for blacks either to reside or to obtain work in white areas but this was not enough for Malan and Verwoerd. They intended to return the blacks to their respective tribal reserves and to destroy the education system for blacks to prevent them from being capable of doing anything other than manual work in the service of the white man.

Malan and Verwoerd did not intend the blacks to have any influence or political rights within the white South African political system but they did support the idea of black self-government within the black tribal reserves. Some areas of South Africa lent themselves to the creation of ethnic territorial units such as the concentration of the Xhosa in the Transkei region of the Eastern Cape or the large concentration of the Zulus in Natal. However, if South African blacks were to be given separate states on a tribal or ethnic basis, then the size of such territorial units would at least have to correspond to the size of that black group as a proportion of the South African population. Such a territory would also have meant that blacks were given good land and that their tribal reserves were capable of sustaining the numbers that lived there.

The major study which looked at the black tribal reserves was the Tomlinson Report, which was completed in 1956 and initially concluded that the tribal reserves were only capable of supporting around a fifth of the black population. As this proportion was considered to be too low, the commission revised its figures and decided that the reserves were capable of supporting just over 50 per cent of the black population. However, these reserves were not contiguous but were scattered and consisted of most of the worst agricultural areas. The Tomlinson Commission therefore recommended that the reserves be expanded in terms of territory and that a significant increase in investment be made in these areas so that they should be able to support a larger population. Despite the continuous opposition and protests from blacks, the National government continued and intensified its policy of forced removals under the apartheid legislation.

In 1954 Malan retired and was replaced as Prime Minister by J. G. Strijdom. Malan had not wanted Strijdom to succeed him as leader of the National Party but he was unable to prevent it. Strijdom was a more strident Nationalist than Malan and was determined to speed up the implementation of apartheid. It was Strijdom who finally brought about the elimination of the coloured franchise in the Cape, which Malan had been attempting to do since 1951. (The coloureds had shared the vote with the whites since the Cape had become self-governing in the previous century.) In order to ensure that such drastic constitutional change was carried out with the minimum of obstruction, Strijdom and the National Party increased the number of like-minded judges in the Appeal Court and in the Senate to guarantee that they had the necessary majorities in both arenas. Then they introduced the legislation disenfranchising the coloured people. During Strijdom's term in office, further measures were introduced which restricted the rights of blacks in educational, cultural and entertainment spheres.

Strijdom died in 1958 and Dr H. F. Verwoerd succeeded him as Prime Minister, a post he occupied until his assassination in 1966. Verwoerd's term in office was marked by growing international and domestic opposition to the policies of racial discrimination. There was growing international criticism of South Africa from the newly independent black African states, India and even the white countries of the British Commonwealth. In 1960 Harold Macmillan, the British Prime Minister, sounded a warning note in his 'wind of change' speech to the

South African parliament. He told the South Africans that policies of overt racism could not be condoned by Britain and that blacks could not be permanently disenfranchised.

Although Verwoerd was annoyed at Macmillan's speech, he restated the determination of the whites to keep control of South Africa and the belief that the blacks were not ready for political power. Macmillan's condemnation of apartheid emphasized the problems that South Africa would face if membership of the British Commonwealth was maintained. For his part, Verwoerd was quite happy both to leave the Commonwealth and to make South Africa a republic and, in 1960, he called a referendum to decide the issue. The result was hardly surprising. There was a majority in favour of South Africa becoming a republic outside the Commonwealth in three of the provinces with only Natal having a majority of voters against.

All South Africa's Prime Ministers had coveted the British High Commission Territories of Basutoland, Bechuanaland and Swaziland and had sought to bring these lands under Pretoria's control. However, by 1960, it had become clear that these territories would not be given to Pretoria and would in

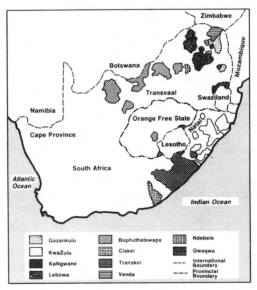

Figure 2   South Africa's Homelands and Independent States

fact become independent black-ruled states. Recognizing that something had to be done to improve South Africa's image in the face of both internal and external criticism, Verwoerd decided to promote the idea of the black homelands becoming not just self-governing areas but independent political states.

Therefore, although blacks would not have rights in the white areas, they would in fact have full freedom in their homelands. The blacks, however, were given no say in the matter and the key decisions were taken exclusively by the National Party. Although black resistance to apartheid grew under Verwoerd, especially from the African National Congress and the Pan-Africanist Congress, the security police quickly broke the armed wings of these respective parties. International criticism was focused on South Africa following the Sharpeville incident in 1960, when some fifty-six blacks were killed and 160 injured during protests against the pass laws.

The assasination of Verwoerd in 1966 left the National Party without an obvious heir. Verwoerd had been one of the most prominent thinkers among the Afrikaner élite and he had an enormous personal following. He had been the driving force behind the vision of grand apartheid, the idea of the total separation of races and it was he who had taken South Africa out of the British Commonwealth and established the republic. This was seen by many Afrikaners as the replay of the Anglo-Boer War, only this time with a Boer victory. The republic had been achieved, the Afrikaner language had been preserved, the Afrikaners had not only taken over the civil service and the military but were also becoming more powerful in commerce.

Verwoerd was succeeded by B. J. Vorster, an advocate, who had been Minister of Justice under Verwoerd since 1962. Vorster had been interned during the 1939–45 war for his membership of the Nazi group, the Ossewa Brandweg. He had made his reputation as a tough Justice Minister and a shrewd political operator. As Justice Minister, it was Vorster who supervised the prosecution of Nelson Mandela and the other leaders of the African National Congress in the early 1960s. With many of their leaders arrested, such as Mandela, Mbeki and Sisulu, or in exile, such as Slovo and Tambo, the ANC opposition was effectively silenced for almost a decade.

Vorster soon realized that the international hostility towards South Africa was growing and that his government needed to do something about it. Along with key advisers, such as van den Bergh, the head of the Bureau of State Security, Vorster attempted to improve relations with the pro-Western and anti-communist states, such as Malawi, Togo and the Ivory Coast. He even made overtures to Zambia in order to discuss the problem of Rhodesia, where the whites had broken with Britain and formed a rebel regime. However, there was a limit as to how far any African state would go in its relations with Pretoria while the discriminatory apartheid laws remained in force.

The South African intervention in Angola in 1975 against the Cuban-supported MPLA wrecked Vorster's attempt to win friends in black Africa. In addition, relations gradually worsened between South Africa and the United States and Britain. The repression of the Soweto protests in 1976 further alienated public opinion in Europe and North America, as did the subsequent death in police custory of Steve Biko, the leader of the Black Consciousness Movement. Another blow to Voster's foreign policy came with the implementation of the United Nations arms embargo in 1977. This measure prohibited the sale of all weapons to the South African government, although ways were found to circumvent this ban.

Vorster had more success in encouraging the growth of self-government in the black homelands. The previous official studies into the situation in the homelands, such as the Tomlinson Commission, had underestimated the demographic increase in the black population and hence the resources in the homelands were increasingly unable to sustain their populations. The Transkei, under Kaiser Matanzima, moved from being a self-governing homeland to an independent state in 1976. Several of the other homelands were also to become independent states in due course. In 1977 Bophuthatswana was to follow suit, Venda in 1979, and the Ciskei in 1981. However, none of the homelands were to receive any international recognition. Other homeland leaders, such as Gatsha Buthelezi, the Chief Minister of KwaZulu, refused to accept what they saw as sham independence. He continued to use his position as Chief Minister of KwaZulu to attack apartheid and to build up the strength of his Inkatha movement.

Faced with rising domestic opposition on a number of

fronts, Vorster appointed the Theron Commission, which made a number of moves towards improving the position of the coloured population. These reforms were poor compensation for the forced removals and disenfranchisement that the coloureds had suffered under the National Party since 1948.

Vorster and Botha's Report

In 1975 Vorster appointed a cabinet committee under P. W. Botha in order to consider possible constitutional reforms. It was initially intended that Botha's report would be used as part of a manifesto for the 1977 general election. Yet several matters prevented this outcome. First, South Africa's deteriorating external relations following the action of the security forces in putting down the township riots in Soweto and other black areas. Second, fearing losses to the left, Vorster decided to fight the 1977 election on the basis of external interference in the internal affairs of South Africa. The external interference was from the usual coalition of troublesome blacks, American and European liberals and, of course, communists.

The report recommended separate parliaments each for the coloureds and Asians. It also recommended moving away from the Westminster-style parliamentary democracy towards a more presidential system with a multi-racial President's Council for advisory purposes. Once the report had been completed, Vorster left it to gather dust. However, P. W. Botha and his supporters believed that the report was the way forward for the reform of the apartheid system of government. An attempt was made to enact some of these proposals in 1979 but it was abandoned for several reasons. First, there were political considerations in the form of a regrouping of disgruntled members of the far right in the National Party, which Botha was determined to keep in check. Second, the implications and ramifications of the legislation had not been fully appreciated and it was not until the 1980s when Botha's reform proposals were passed into law.

As South Africa grew more isolated, Vorster realized the importance of reforming apartheid. Yet even minor concessions, such as allowing integrated sport, brought forth trenchant attacks from the right wing of the National Party. In 1969 a group of these diehards led by Albert Hertzog formed the Herstigte Nasionale Party (Restructured National Party), but the right-wing opposition to the National Party was not to be a major threat until the 1980s with the challenge from the Conservative Party. As his problems mounted, Vorster's health declined. He had seen his country become more isolated internationally, and the buffer states along South Africa's borders, apart from Rhodesia, were ruled by black governments and even there, it was only a matter of time. There was serious internal unrest following the Soweto disturbances in 1976 and a growth in assassinations and bombings by the African National Congress. In 1978 Vorster became State President but he resigned within two years because of his involvement in the Information scandal. He died soon afterwards.

Chapter 2

THE RISE OF P. W. BOTHA

Throughout the 1970s, Vorster faced mounting political difficulties at home and abroad. He had launched his détente initiative with some of the more pro-Western African states and it appeared that this might meet with some success. However, the South African intervention in Angola and the subsequent reneging on promises of help by the Western powers, especially the United States, left Vorster feeling bitter and betrayed. His domestic difficulties mounted in 1976 with the Soweto protests and the hostile international response to their repression. The death of the Black Consciousness leader, Steve Biko, in police custody in 1977 led to further international criticism of the South African government. Vorster was ill and it was obvious to his colleagues that he would not continue as Prime Minister for much longer.

There were two major rivals for the leadership of the National Party. Dr Connie Mulder, the Minister of Information and leader of the National Party in the Transvaal, and P. W. Botha, the Minister of Defence and leader of the National Party in the Cape. The Transvaal tended to be a more conservative area, while the Cape tended by tradition to be a more liberal province. In 1978 Vorster resigned as Prime Minister and was elected State President and a struggle ensued for the party leadership at the National Party conference between Dr Mulder, P. W. Botha and R.F. 'Pik' Botha, the Foreign Minister. On the first ballot, Dr Mulder secured a majority over P. W. Botha but not by a large enough margin. On the second ballot, the votes for R.F. Botha were transferred to P. W. Botha, thus ensuring his victory for the leadership. Throughout 1977 rumours had abounded of the involvement of Mulder's department in irregular financial dealings. These rumours contributed to the decision of a number of Mulder's supporters not to vote for him.

The Information Scandal

Dr Connie Mulder, the leading figure in the Transvaal Nationalist Party, was Vorster's Minister for Information.

Mulder's department had been responsible for a number of clandestine projects that were aimed at neutralizing anti-government propaganda. Among these was buying newspapers both at home and abroad. In South Africa the Department of Information attempted to purchase several newspapers that had traditionally been read by English-speakers and blacks, with the aim of feeding pro-government propaganda to a traditionally unsympathetic audience.

A number of rumours began to circulate in 1976 that there was extensive abuse of public funds by the Department of Information. Government auditors became concerned at the way money was spent by the department and in particular on matters involving exchange control, but it was not until November 1978 that serious legal enquiries were made into the activities of the department. Judge Mostert, who had been assigned the task of investigating irregularities on exchange control, became extremely concerned about some of the transactions carried out by the Department of Information and made some of his concerns known to the press.

P. W. Botha, by now Prime Minister, decided to wind up the Mostert Commission and to set up a new enquiry under Judge Erasmus, to investigate the Department of Information. In his initial report, Judge Erasmus concluded that the former Prime Minister and State President B. J. Vorster had not known about the misuse of public funds under the Department of Information but that Dr Connie Mulder had known of it.

Mulder argued that Vorster and van den Bergh had both known about the Department of Information's covert projects and his charges led Judge Erasmus to revise his conclusions to state that Vorster had been aware of the financial irregularities associated with the secret projects. As a result of the report Dr Eschel Rhoodie, the Secretary of the Department, was charged with a number of offences and although initially convicted he was acquitted on appeal.

The Information scandal was christened 'Muldergate' in the popular press and it was to have consequences for the realignment of Afrikanerdom in the 1980s. Mulder was to leave the National Party, van den Bergh was to retire to his farm and his Bureau of State Security (BOSS) was reorganized and lost much of its power. On the other hand, P. W. Botha was strengthened just as his main rival for the leadership of the National Party was outcast.

Botha in Charge

The conclusions of the Erasmus Report allowed P. W. Botha not only to get rid of possible opponents, such as Mulder and van den Bergh from the higher echelons of government, but also enabled him to carry out a number of reforms that strengthened his position within the government. BOSS was reorganized and the Department of Military Intelligence became the key agency for advising Botha. Botha's years first as Prime Minister and then as State President were marked by a shift of power away from the legislature and towards the executive. In part this was due to Botha's autocratic character but in part also to his belief that in order to carry out his programme of constitutional reform, it would be necessary to reduce the power of the more militant back-benchers.

The reform of the apartheid regime inevitably meant opposition from those who benefited most by its practices, namely the white working class. Pressure for reforms came not only from the disenfranchised black opposition but also from many sectors in the business community, who found the costs of apartheid to be a major brake on economic growth as well as a problem in overseas markets. The removal of job reservation, the laws on interracial marriage and sexual liaisons, relaxations in the Group Areas Act and the giving of the vote to the coloured and Asian populations all met with resistance from the Afrikaner *verkramptes* (reactionaries).

The constitutional changes introduced by P. W. Botha were revolutionary and marked the beginning of the end of the era of white supremacy. Botha reckoned that the loss of white minority rule in Rhodesia in 1980 meant that there were potentially hostile countries along all of South Africa's northern borders, while a guerrilla war continued in South African-occupied Namibia (formerly South-West Africa). An international arms embargo deprived South Africa of external supplies of weapons and the international isolation of the republic was growing. Furthermore, the South Africans perceived that the Soviet Union and its allies were considering increased support for both the ANC and the South-West Africa People's Organization (SWAPO), the guerrilla movement in Namibia. Political reform was therefore a matter of extreme urgency for P. W. Botha and his government.

27

The central problem for Botha was to decide what direction he should follow with his programme of reforms. How could the National Party begin to share power with the other political groups in South Africa? One option was for the National Party to try and split the coloureds and Asians away from the blacks by granting them the franchise. The National Party would then try and build an anti-ANC alliance between the whites, the coloureds, the Asians and the black homeland leaders. The blacks could then be given the franchise within the context of their homelands and white political and economic power would remain intact.

This strategy was unlikely to succeed for a number of reasons: first, the coloureds and Indians would not go along with it, nor would Chief Buthelezi, the leader of Inkatha and the Chief Minister of KwaZulu. Second, the whites were unwilling to redivide the land so as to ensure that the blacks at least controlled an amount of territory in line with their percentage of the South African population. Without a major redivision of land to make the homelands viable and contiguous territories, any strategy based on the homelands was doomed to fail. Third, economic and demographic factors were making such a scenario even less likely. Urbanization and economic growth were moving the black population out of the homelands and into the white heartlands.

A second option for the South African government was to try and build a series of local power-sharing experiments based on regional rather than ethnic divisions. This strategy was recommended by Chief Buthelezi, many of the white opposition groups and academics following the Natal indaba (conference). Buthelezi was popular with the white community in Natal because of his staunch anti-communist views and many people saw the indaba as an imaginative attempt to move forward away from apartheid. The National government did not feel it could go along with the indaba's suggestions because it feared that there were not enough safeguards for the white community. A more likely explanation of its opposition to the power-sharing project was that it was not yet prepared to give up any meaningful degree of power to the black opposition and it feared its success might lead to the blacks demanding similar projects in other parts of South Africa.

A third option was the radical position of dealing directly

with the leaders of the ANC in negotiations with a relatively open-ended agenda, which amounted to an effective rejection of National Party policies since 1948. This policy involved the release of Nelson Mandela and other ANC veterans, the unbanning of the ANC, the South African Communist Party and the PAC, and the release of other political prisoners before the ANC would even begin talking to the National government.

With the growing threat from the Afrikaner right, P.W. Botha was unable to pursue either the second or the third options. Botha was vainly trying to follow the first option until he stood down as State President, by which time it was obvious that the policy was a dismal failure. F.W. de Klerk, on the other hand, was to pursue option three immediately upon taking over from Botha as State President.

Botha's first move towards reform was to alter the constitution to give more power to the State President and the executive. The President was to be elected by an electoral college, which was designed so as to give the major white party (i.e. the National Party) the greatest say. Once he had accomplished this, he went on to announce the setting up of a tricameral parliament with separate representation for the coloureds in the House of Representatives and for the Indians in the House of Delegates, which came into effect in 1984. Further reforms were intended for local government and the townships but these were to run into major problems over both the question of forced removals and the eruption of popular protests in the townships in 1984.

Botha's reform programme failed because it was too little and too late. The electoral turn-out for the coloured and Indian elections was very low (i.e. a 31 per cent turn-out for the coloured electorate; a 24 per cent turn-out for the Indian electorate), thus casting doubt on their legitimacy and the issue of political representation for the blacks was ignored. The black reaction to Botha's new constitution was extremely hostile and led to widespread anti-government violence in the townships. Caught between a growing challenge from the right from the Conservative Party and the Afrikaner Weerstandsbeweging (AWB) and from growing black unrest on the left, Botha attempted to appease the right and repress the left but ended up failing to achieve either objective.

In response to the unrest in the townships in 1984, the

Botha government declared a state of emergency in some areas the following year, imposed tough public order legislation, strict controls on the press and sent the army into the townships. Reform slowed down on the key issue of the franchise for blacks, although in 1985 the National government abolished the laws which forbade interracial marriage and interracial sexual liaisons.

The Conservative Opposition

Opposition from the right wing of the Afrikaner community was by no means unique to P. W. Botha: the first stirrings of disapproval of Nationalist government policies came in the 1970s, from Hertzog's Herstigte Nasionale Party. Opposition was focused on two levels: on the one hand, it was targeted at de facto policies of reform under Vorster, such as policies aimed at dismantling petty apartheid; and on the other, criticism was levelled at any abandonment of the Verwoerdian vision of grand apartheid. This opposition was to grow in the 1980s and was to find a large electoral constituency in the new Conservative Party, led by Dr Andries Treurnicht, himself a former government minister under P. W. Botha.

In the 1987 general election the Conservative Party took 29.2 per cent of the popular vote and twenty-two of the 166 seats in the House of Assembly. These results tended to underestimate the size of Conservative support because the National Party gained 122 seats with 51 per cent of the popular vote. The South African voting system tended to favour the National Party against its opponents because the South African constituencies were weighted in favour of the rural and against the urban areas. Initially, rural areas had supported the National Party against the United Party of Smuts, but as the Conservative Party began to find favour with rural voters, the advantage that once helped the Nationalists could now work against them. The Conservative Party was founded in February 1982, when Treurnicht and fifteen others resigned from the National Party. They left because they were opposed not only to P. W. Botha's programme of constitutional reform but also to the concept of power-sharing with any section of the non-white population. The party gathered support from those who felt that they had the most to lose from any growth in power by the other ethnic groups in South Africa, such as poor whites in the civil service bureaucracy, who feared that the growing influence of the blacks would lead to fewer jobs for them. Some feared that under a future black government they might suffer job losses. Support for the Conservatives was also strong among the skilled Afrikaner working class, who had an important stake in job reservation. These were poor whites, who depended on pay differentials or job reservation: in other words discrimination based on race to prevent non-whites competing with them in the labour market.

Although the National Party had traditionally stressed the common interests of all white Afrikaners, it had gone out of its way to help the poor Afrikaners in order to mobilize them as an electoral constituency. As South Africa faced growing economic difficulties and the need to make concessions to the black population in order to stimulate economic growth, so it had less need for the restrictive and discriminatory policies espoused by the poor whites. In fact, such policies were a hindrance and detrimental to economic growth.

Geographically, the Conservative Party had its strength in the rural areas of the Orange Free State and the Transvaal, but in the 1987 election it showed that it could also secure support in the urban areas of the Pretoria-Witwatersrand-Vereeniging (PWV) triangle and here its vote was from the working-class districts. The timing of the rise in support for the Conservative Party was also significant. A realignment in the social base of the National Party was taking place and the party no longer represented the interests of all classes of Afrikaners. The National Party was beginning to reflect the views of the more affluent Afrikaners, whose views on political and economic reform had begun to move closer to those of the English-speakers. The National Party was also gaining the support of more English-speakers as it moved towards reforming apartheid. This meant that economic growth and political stability were more important than the interests of the poor whites.

Economic growth required reduction in labour costs, foreign investment, the rapid deployment of new technology and access to foreign markets. In the 1970s and 1980s, the apartheid policies endangered each of these requirements: the costs of job reservation and a migrant workforce added to labour costs, while new technology was often withheld from South Africa because of sanctions. Therefore sustaining apartheid was at the cost of consumer boycotts of South

African exports, increasing problems in gaining access to foreign markets, and growing difficulties in obtaining new loans and new technology, all of which impeded economic growth. Low productivity put South Africa at a further disadvantage.

As the Group Areas Act was relaxed, so poor whites had to compete for housing with their more affluent non-white rivals. The ending of job reservation for a number of skilled and supervisory positions meant that non-whites were becoming a more important source of competition in the field of employment. In terms of status, the poor whites were also under threat. In the days of grand apartheid, being white meant being part of the ruling group and even the poorest of that ruling group had many advantages over the other 80+ per cent of the South African population. It meant reserved areas to live, certain jobs reserved for whites only as of right and a whole baasskap culture by which the non-whites were obliged to acknowledge their inferior status, thus inflating that of the poor whites. The reforms of Botha and de Klerk struck not only at the economic and political privileges of the poor whites but also at their status benefits, which were then assuming more importance because of the decline of the other benefits of being white.

Among the farming community there was also growing resentment against the Botha reforms during the early 1980s. A severe drought in 1982 caused hardship to the rural population, although some sectors of agriculture were hurt more than others. The small farmers in the Orange Free State and the Transvaal fared much worse than the large-scale farmers in the Cape and Natal. The Conservative Party had an initial advantage in that the head of the Broederbond, Dr Carel Boshoff, was sympathetic to their cause and many of the front organizations of the Broederbond were also more sympathetic to the Conservative Verwoerdian programme than to the reforms of P. W. Botha. In response, the National Party rapidly reorganized and won back control of the Broederbond and its major front groups. In the Dutch Reformed Churches there was also bitter acrimony over support for the new party but many of the more stridently Calvinist clergy were more in tune with the Conservatives than the National Party.

The disturbances in the black townships and the national

state of emergency imposed in 1986 also helped the Conservative Party, as poor whites demanded that the unrest be crushed by force of arms, regardless of the casualties that might be inflicted on the black population. However, other factors indicated that the Conservative Party had reached its maximal level of support. In areas where the Conservatives took control of local and municipal councils, they reintroduced measures of petty apartheid with disastrous results. In Boksburg, the local blacks, using tactics copied from the United States civil rights movement, organized a buyers' boycott of white-owned shops practising apartheid. This led to a drastic fall in trade and made the whites question the wisdom of Conservative policies.

The Conservative Party's major policies for the future of South Africa contain one major weakness. Their fundamental objection to the National Party is a rejection of the concept of power-sharing with the other ethnic groups, who comprise 86 per cent of the South African population. Clinging to the Verwoerdian concept of separate development, the Conservatives would rather partition South Africa into a number of states with the whites (especially the Afrikaners) keeping control of one state.

They argue that power-sharing with the other ethnic groups will only lead to the destruction of the white identity in South Africa, therefore it would be better for whites to give up sections of South African territory to the blacks, in order to keep one area under total white political control. The Conservative Party views South Africa as ten black nations, the whites, the coloureds and the Indians and each of these nations should have its own separate state. The African states should be extensions of the existing homelands, the coloureds should have their state in the Cape province where they are traditionally concentrated, while the Indians should have their state in Natal. The white population were to retain control of the major population centres and the country's economic wealth. They would revert to having a parliamentary democracy with a whites-only franchise.

The increasing economic and demographic integration of the South African population, however, has made the idea of separation impractical and unworkable. None of the major economic interests in South Africa favours partition, nor do any of the black opposition groups. Conservative Party policies appeal to only a minority of the white population and, after their failure in local councils under Conservative control, seem unlikely to increase their support.

Other White Opposition

Many whites, including Afrikaners, shared neither the National Party's vision of apartheid as the most desirable future for South Africa, nor that of the Conservative Party. For many years after 1948, the United Party continued to criticize the National Party, condemning both apartheid and the corruption that seemed to haunt the National Party's period in government. The growing affluence of the white community in the 1960s led many of the English-speakers reluctantly to accept apartheid. If the Afrikaners were monopolizing political power and jobs in the public sector (the civil service and the military), many English-speaking whites were doing very well in the private sector. There did not seem to be a middle way between maintaining white political and economic power through apartheid and majority rule as demanded by the black opposition groups. Most whites believed that this would inevitably lead to a loss of their political and economic power and hence was undesirable.

If the United Party were to regain the support of more whites it could not offer too many concessions to the black opposition, without which, however, it would be unable to gain black support. Those on the liberal wing of the United Party, such as Helen Suzman, moved to the Progressive Party, while the more conservative wing formed the New Republic Party.

The Progressive Party was formed in 1959 as a breakaway group from the United Party. In 1975 it was renamed the Progressive Reform Party which it remained until 1977, when it became the Progressive Federal Party. The Progressive Party drew its support from the more affluent English-speaking community and it was also to receive support from several of the large mining houses. For many years its sole representative in parliament was Helen Suzman. In 1977 the Progressive Federal Party (PFP) was led by Colin Eglin but in 1979 he was replaced as leader by the charismatic Dr Frederick Van Zyl Slabbert. Dr Van Zyl Slabbert was a strident critic of Botha's constitutional reforms and in 1986 he resigned from parliament because he believed that he could carry on a more useful role in opposition by organizing bridge-building exercises between the white community and the exiled black opposition groups, especially the ANC.

In 1987 Van Zyl Slabbert organized a series of meetings between leading Afrikaner businessmen and academics and members of the ANC. These exchanges were useful to all parties as a forum in which to explore possible areas of common ground and to facilitate the potential for peaceful change in South Africa.

The PFP believed in a decentralized South Africa, where power would be devolved on a geographic rather than an ethnic basis. Inevitably, such division would have a certain element of ethnic base: the Zulus would always be dominant in Natal and the Xhosas in the Transkei. However, a coalition government would be essential for the long-term stability of South Africa. The essence of a coalition or consociational form of government was that all the major parties would be represented in cabinet positions in the central government.

In the 1987 general election, the PFP gained twenty seats with 15.6 per cent of the popular vote. When matters of national security or public order were the central issues on the political agenda, the white electorate preferred policies that stressed a restoration of order rather than policies that stressed reforms and negotiations with South Africa's black majority. As the National Party was pushing through a number of reforms, many more English-speakers were prepared to support it in order to keep the Conservative Party out of power. The National Party was seen by many whites as the only realistic agency of reform in the short term despite the fact that many in the upper echelons of the National Party were more preoccupied with the threat from the conservative right than from either the liberal left or the black opposition. The reason for this was that the National Party leadership, especially P. W. Botha, did not wish to split Afrikanerdom as had happened in the inter-war years. The black unrest could be contained by the security forces by means of repression and stringent public order legislation but a split in Afrikanerdom could threaten the dominance of the National Party in government.

Even within the National Party there were growing signs of division among the Afrikaner élite. The traditional cleavage in the Afrikaner community was between the *verligte* (enlightened) and the *verkrampte* (reactionary) but these divisions were not absolute. Many *verkramptes* remained within the National Party after the secession of others to the Conservative Party in 1982. The *verligtes*, on the other hand, covered a range of views within the National Party but also included people who supported the PFP.

The division among the *verligtes* became more intense in the mid-1980s, when the Botha government slowed the pace of its reforms and concentrated on suppressing the unrest in the townships. Some *verligtes* wanted the government to move faster towards reforms and threatened to split off from the National Party. Botha feared moving further to the left because he was more concerned about losses to the right and the Conservative Party if he did embark on more concessions to the blacks.

The signal for the realignment of the left wing of the white community was the return of South Africa's ambassador to Britain, Dr Denis Worrall, to stand for the Helderburg constituency in the Cape for the 1987 election. Worrall's opponent was none other than J.C. Heunis, P.W. Botha's heir-apparent. Although Worrall was unable to oust Heunis, he ran him so close that Heunis was discredited as a future leader of the National Party. Worrall joined forces with other liberal figures in the Afrikaner community, such as Wynand Malan and later Frederick Van Zyl Slabbert, to form the Democratic Party in 1989.

The Democratic Party faced tactical problems in its attempt to increase its support. If the Democrats were to eat into the National Party's support, then they would have to move to the right, but not only would they risk losing support on the left but they would also move away from the black opposition groups. If the Democratic Party was to move to the left, then it was unlikely to increase its vote among the white community and so would lose its influence for conciliation between the white community and the black opposition.

Botha's Achievements

By 1988 Botha had become a spent volcano: he was ill and he felt that he could offer little in the way of reforms to the blacks without seeing the further division of the Afrikaner community. The major black groups had become so alienated from Botha following the 1983 constitution which set up the tricameral parliament that no amount of concessions would have restored their trust in him. Botha had managed to make a start towards the reform of apartheid: he abolished many of the petty apartheid laws and brought representatives from the coloured and Asian populations back into parliament. Although Botha had increased the power of the executive, he had done so in order to force through a number of reforms that it might otherwise have been difficult to achieve. Even the ideas of total onslaught (see Chapter 3) had more importance for mobilizing the white community and pressurizing it into accepting change and reform than as a coherent counter-insurgency doctrine.

Botha's achievements in foreign policy are more difficult to measure. His liberal Foreign Minister, R. F. 'Pik' Botha, and his conservative Defence Minister, Magnus Malan, often seemed to be pursuing conflicting policies. By 1984, South African military power and support for anti-communist insurgents in Angola and Mozambique had forced both countries to negotiate peace terms with Pretoria. Furthermore, both these countries promised to withdraw sanctuary for guerrillas fighting against the South African government.

On the other hand, within five years, the South Africans had had to negotiate with both the ANC and SWAPO. Was the military effort worth the cost? The use of South African military power had also led to greater superpower involvement in southern Africa that in turn had led to the military balance tipping away from South Africa in favour of the frontline states. Although Botha had gone a long way towards reform in comparison to any of his forebears, his greatest failure was his inability to offer meaningful political reform to South African blacks.

De Klerk and Reform

From the mid-1980s, P.W. Botha showed increasing signs of ill-health and rumours began to circulate about his retirement. Two candidates were favoured as the future leader of the National Party, J.C. Heunis and F.W. de Klerk. At first, Heunis was considered to be the more likely victor in the leadership contest. He had held a number of key appointments, including Minister of Constitutional Development. On the other hand, F.W. de Klerk had also held a number of important offices, such as Minister of the Interior, Minister of

Mineral and Energy Affairs and Minister for Education. However, Heunis suffered in 1987 from his election contest with Dr Denis Worrall and also from his association with the tricameral constitution. As the leader of the National Party in the Transvaal, de Klerk had a strong power base within the party and emerged as P. W. Botha's heir.

Other possible candidates for the leadership of the National Party either lacked enough support from the rank and file of the party or were not seen as being able to keep the National Party united. For example, R. F. Botha, the Minister for Foreign Affairs, was seen as too liberal, while those such as Magnus Malan, the Minister of Defence, were seen as being too conservative and lacking enough support among the party grassroots.

Despite further illness in 1988, Botha was reluctant to give up the reins of political office. His leadership was to end on a sour note following a row with de Klerk over a visit to Zambia.

Once in power as State President, de Klerk rapidly moved to reduce the role and influence of the military, which had been so pervasive under P. W. Botha's leadership, and contacted prominent leaders in the West in order to spell out his plans for the future reform of South Africa.

De Klerk impressed not only Western leaders such as Mrs Thatcher but also Dr Kenneth Kaunda, the Zambian leader. Most South African leaders began their tenure of office with the promise of reforms but few went on to carry out such promises. F W. de Klerk was the exception. In 1990 de Klerk ordered the release of Nelson Mandela, one of the imprisoned leaders of the ANC, and he announced a further series of reforms that included the unbanning of the ANC, the South African Communist Party and the PAC, along with the ending of restrictions on many other anti-apartheid activists. In addition to this, discussions began between the National Party and the ANC on the question of black political rights. A number of prominent figures in the National Party indicated that key pieces of apartheid legislation, such as the Group Areas Act, would be repealed in the near future and that the principle of universal franchise for all ethnic groups in South Africa was accepted. In the summer of 1990 the ANC suspended its armed struggle against the Pretoria government as negotiations got under way towards a peaceful resolution of the South African conflict.

Chapter 3

FOREIGN AND DEFENCE POLICY

South African foreign and defence policy since 1945 has been marked by the search for allies and security. However, successive Nationalist governments have faced increasing international opposition and hostility to their domestic policies of apartheid.

Since the end of the Second World War, South Africa has been the dominant military power on the African continent. Smuts, the South African Prime Minister from 1939 to 1948, was a respected international statesman who played a prominent role in the founding of the United Nations in 1945. Yet the United Nations were soon to provide a forum for critics of the South African government's policies on racial matters.

Prior to the Second World War, South African foreign policy had followed that of Britain in its outlook, but this was to change with the gradual British withdrawal from its empire. However, two factors were to lead the South African government in different directions from the British. The first was the Nationalist victory in the 1948 general election, which led to the Afrikanerization of most of the senior administrative, military and diplomatic posts as Afrikaners quickly replaced the English-speaking personnel in the higher echelons of government service. Second, as more of the apartheid policies were passed into law, so international hostility to the South African government increased. The policies of apartheid embarrassed Britain with its other Commonwealth allies and led to a gradual rift between the two countries. Third, many of the National Party leadership wanted to make South Africa a republic and so reduce British influence.

Fourth, there was the decision of the major European powers in the 1950s and early 1960s to grant self-government to their African colonies. As the British states became independent, so the British empire became the British Commonwealth and many of these newly independent countries were black-ruled and unwilling to consider that South Africa should be allowed to remain as a part of the Commonwealth. Matters came to a head following the visit of the British Prime Minister Harold Macmillan to South Africa in 1960. He gave his famous 'wind of change' speech to a joint session of both houses of parliament in Cape Town, in which he argued that the political power of the newly independent states was growing and that the aspirations of the new African populations could not be ignored. His warning was particularly aimed at the Afrikaners because of their policies of discrimination towards the non-white ethnic groups in South Africa.

Macmillan went on to warn the leaders of the National Party both publicly and privately that they must make allowances for the Africans within their own country and treat them as equal citizens. The speech was intended as a timely warning to old friends but was met with disgust from the National Party leaders, who resented this representative of British imperialism telling them how to deal with their native problem. Dr Verwoerd, the Prime Minister, was among those Afrikaners who believed that this was the time to consider making the break with the Commonwealth and establishing a republic. Backed by his lieutenants, such as Henning Klopper, one of the most important leaders of the Broederbond, Verwoerd called a referendum on the issue of the republic. The result was a majority in Verwoerd's favour although had the coloureds still had the franchise (lost in the mid-1950s) such a result would have been unlikely.

The break from the Commonwealth was inevitable because South Africa's policies of racial discrimination against blacks had become untenable within the Commonwealth and even the other white-ruled states such as Canada, Australia and New Zealand were opposed to such discrimination and to South African membership of the Commonwealth while such policies were practised.

Britain and South Africa were soon to have differences on another issue, the decolonization of the Rhodesian Federation. There was a large white settler population in the Rhodesian Federation but the largest section of it was concentrated in Southern Rhodesia. The settler population in Southern Rhodesia wanted an independent state in which they, not the emerging black élite, would have control of political and economic power. In 1964, as the date for reaching an independence agreement for the federation drew nearer, the settlers aligned themselves behind the Rhodesia Front Party and its new leader Ian Smith. The leadership of the Rhodesia Front wished to move towards a unilateral declaration of independence; they knew that the British government would not recognize the white minority government, but they also knew that Britain would be unable to intervene to stop them. (The other components of the federation, Northern Rhodesia and Nyasaland, became independent as Zambia and Malawi respectively.)

The Rhodesians knew that the Portuguese were unlikely to be hostile to their moves towards independence and that the surrounding black-ruled states would be too weak to do anything about it. However, the key factor was South Africa. As Rhodesia was landlocked and was dependent on oil imports, it was important that it could guarantee the support of its neighbours, especially its southern one. The Rhodesian black nationalist opposition was ill-prepared to take on the power of the settler security forces and the guerrilla movement was heavily penetrated with informers.

The guerrilla struggle against the Portuguese empire was slightly better organized but varied between Mozambique and Angola. In Mozambique, the Frente da Libertação de Moçambique (Frelimo) was the major guerrilla force but it was tribally dominated by the Makondes, while the guerrilla forces in Angola were divided along ethnic and ideological lines. The Frente Nacional da Libertação de Angola (FNLA) was led by Holden Roberto and supported by the Kongo tribe in the north of Angola which comprised 14 per cent of the population. They were supported by Zaire and occasionally by other pro-Western countries. The União Nacional para a Independência Total de Angola (UNITA) was led by Jonas Savimbi and supported by the Ovimbundu, who comprise 38 per cent of the Angolan population. They were originally supported by the Chinese but eventually were assisted by a coalition of countries including France, Morocco, Saudi Arabia, the United States and South Africa. The group that was eventually put in power by the Cuban army was the Movimento Populare para a Libertação de Angola (MPLA) which was led by Agostinho Neto and supported by the Mbundu tribe, the half-castes and the communists. Geographically, their strength was in the centre of Angola and in the main coastal towns, including the capital, Luanda.

Although clinging to its African empire, Portugal was one of the poorest countries in Europe and the growing cost of funding a number of counter-insurgency wars further consumed its scarce resources of money and manpower. In 1974 the Portuguese military mounted a coup against the fascist dictatorship of Dr Marcelo Caetano. This was important for the South Africans because the exiled African National Congress was based in Zambia, and its armed wing, MK, faced a long and difficult infiltration route through either Angola and Namibia or through Portuguese-controlled Mozambique from its other rearward bases in Tanzania. Even the South-West Africa People's Organization (SWAPO) had to infiltrate its guerrillas through Angola or via Zambia. The collapse of the Portuguese cordon sanitaire meant that the guerrilla struggles in Namibia and South Africa were likely to get worse. For the Rhodesians, the fall of the Portuguese colony of Mozambique was the beginning of the end. Since 1965 the Rhodesians had had to cover their north-western border with Zambia against guerrilla infiltration, which they had managed to do remarkably well, but after 1973 they also had to cover their long eastern border with Mozambique. This placed an impossible load on the Rhodesian security forces and it was soon clear to senior figures in the Rhodesian government that they would have to come to some form of political settlement with their black population.

The Frelimo takeover in Mozambique also meant that there was likely to be a hostile Marxist government on South Africa's north-eastern border. South African government options to prevent this were very limited but reflected the divisions between two of the three major groups in the South African government that were involved with decision-making in foreign policy matters. These were the Bureau of State Security (BOSS), headed by General Hendrik van den Bergh, the Department of Defence, headed by P.W. Botha and the Department of Foreign Affairs, headed by R.F. 'Pik' Botha. The conflicts between these three groups showed the differences in priorities and strategies held by each group. Van den Bergh was of the opinion that South Africa should remain aloof from military commitments abroad and that the emphasis on controlling the opposition should be done within South African borders and should be the work of the security branch of the South African police and BOSS.

Analysts in the Department of Defence were divided in their views. Some believed that it might be possible to partition Mozambique with the aid of a number of colonists and by an ingathering of whites in the southern provinces of the country along the South African border. This scheme was opposed by both the Department of Foreign Affairs and by van den Bergh. Van den Bergh did not want to see South African involvement in another potential Rhodesia and he was also aware that such an action would seriously violate the Organization of African Unity's (OAU) principle of the inviolability of the old colonial boundaries. This meant that international recognition was unlikely to be forthcoming for any future secessionist state. As Vorster was busy trying to organize his own détente exercise with some of the more conservative African states at that time, the last thing he needed was a military invasion of southern Mozambique or a South African-backed settler secession in southern Mozambique. The Department of Foreign Affairs was also engaged in supporting the détente initiative with Senegal, the Ivory Coast and Zambia and thus opposed any plans for intervention in Mozambique.

The case of Angola was different. As there were three anti-imperialist groups in the liberation movement, the problem of organizing the transition was more problematic for the departing Portuguese. The differences between these groups were reflected not only in ethnic and linguistic terms but also in terms of external support and in a personal animosity between the leaders of the three groups, the FNLA, the MPLA and UNITA. Furthermore, other conservative African leaders such as President Mobutu in Zaire and President Kaunda of Zambia were deeply concerned at the involvement of the Marxist MPLA with the Soviet Union and Cuba. The Portuguese had tried to bring the various Angolan liberation groups together at the Alvor Agreement (1974) but as the Portuguese army withdrew, fighting broke out in Luanda between the FNLA and the MPLA. As the date of independence drew nearer the Marxist MPLA made it clear that it intended to establish a one-party state, despite the fact that it had the support of barely a quarter of the Angolan population.

South African Intervention in Angola

The initial South African intervention in Angola was in August 1975, when an army detachment was sent over the Angolan border to protect South African workers on the Cuenene dam project; in addition, however, a small group of advisers and artillerymen was sent secretly to the north of Angola to help the FNLA. South Africa, the United States, France, Zambia, Zaire and the conservative French-speaking West African states were growing increasingly concerned at the growing Cuban and Soviet involvement in Angola. The FNLA had some external assistance from Zaire but these troops were of very poor quality and, as a result, the FNLA leader Holden Roberto began to recruit mercenaries. The American Central Intelligence Agency (CIA) also organized a small amount of help for the FNLA through its Kinshasa base in Zaire. However the FNLA remained poorly equipped and lacked the manpower to fight its MPLA rivals. The French secret service, the SDECE (Service de Documentation Extérieure et Contre-Espionage) recruited mercenaries for UNITA, which was much larger and both better armed and trained. By far the largest intervention was that of the Cuban and Soviet combat forces.

The United States government and several of the African states were keen to see the South Africans launch an attack to support UNITA in southern Angola against the Cubans and the MPLA. The prospect of a Marxist state with a large force of Cuban and Soviet combat forces on the Namibian border tilted the balance in the South African government in favour of further intervention. The South Africans invaded Angola in three armoured columns in an operation codenamed Savannah but this invasion did not involve a major commitment from the South African Defence Force (SADF). The United States had promised aid but did not want the South African forces to take the Angolan capital of Luanda, while the South African Prime Minister Vorster did not want to commit major South African forces in case the United States should pull out and leave them in the lurch. In particular, Vorster was concerned that any losses of equipment would not be replaced because of possible arms embargoes, the South African air force being especially vulnerable to such sanctions. The South African army smashed through the MPLA but the Cuban dictator, Fidel Castro, rushed reinforcements of men and munitions to Angola. Then the United States Congress, still smarting from the Watergate affair and the US withdrawal from Vietnam, passed the Clark Amendment, which prohibited further American aid to the UNITA forces in Angola. Vorster and van den Bergh's worst scenario had come to pass: South Africa had been encouraged to go out on a limb and had then been deserted by its allies. Furthermore, Vorster's détente policy had been wrecked and South Africa had appeared as an international aggressor.

The Soviet and Cuban presence in Angola tilted the military balance in favour of the MPLA and, despite heavy pressure from other Soviet client states, the OAU did not immediately recognize the MPLA as the lawful government of Angola. The South African military presence in Angola was seen by many African governments as being more offensive than the Cuban and Soviet presence. It seemed that the governments of South Africa, the United States and France had underestimated the reaction of the Soviet Union and Cuba to the escalation of the conflict; consequently, the South African forces withdrew to the Namibian border. For the South Africans, it was a political rather than a military defeat. If they had mobilized the full potential of their military might, they would certainly have defeated the Cuban and MPLA forces. However, none of the black-ruled African states was prepared openly to support South African intervention, nor were the United States, Britain, West Germany and France.

Vorster's détente initiative had been ruined and the MPLA became established as the government of Angola. The South Africans had finally had to face up to the realization that when the crunch came, they were on their own.

The Angolan defeat had both domestic and international ramifications for South Africa. The myth of white military invincibility was shattered and the domestic opposition took heart from the MPLA and Cuban victory in Angola. Second, the Frelimo victory in Mozambique was to bring about a dramatic change in the situation in Rhodesia. The turning-point in the guerrilla struggle was in 1973, when the Zimbabwean African National Liberation Army (ZANLA) forces belonging to ZANU were able to open the second front and infiltrate Rhodesia all along the Mozambican border. The security situation rapidly deteriorated for the Smith government and several of his advisers, such as Ken Flower, the head of the Central Intelligence Organization, urged him to negotiate with some of the black opposition groups inside Rhodesia.

The independence of Mozambique meant that the ANC was also able to infiltrate members into South Africa, while

Angola's independence meant that members of the South-West Africa People's Organization (SWAPO) were able to infiltrate Namibia from bases in southern Angola. So the fall of the Portuguese Lusophone countries led to an escalation of the guerrilla resistance in both Rhodesia and Namibia.

The South Africans had long hoped that they might form the nucleus of a southern hemisphere version of the North Atlantic Treaty Organization (NATO) but their domestic policies of apartheid made them more of a liability to the West. Nevertheless, the South Africans continued to exchange intelligence with the British, French and Americans. They kept several of their key naval facilities available for a future time when the NATO forces might need them and they continued to develop the Silvermine communications centre, which monitored shipping and, in particular, Soviet naval activities in the southern Atlantic and the Indian Ocean.

The South African government was also becoming more isolated at the United Nations not only because of the growing strength of the Third World nations but also because of its support for the white minority regime in Rhodesia and the continuing South African occupation of Namibia. After 1976, two of South Africa's traditional allies began to distance themselves from Pretoria. Although Britain continued to obtain South African assistance to persuade the Rhodesian leader Ian Smith to accept majority rule, the Labour government went along with the United Nations arms embargo and refused to sell the South Africans any more armaments. Subsequently, the French government was to follow suit and cancelled an agreement to supply the Pretoria government with submarines. The South Africans had also traditionally seen the United States as an ally in the struggle against world communism, but with the election of the Democratic candidate for the American presidency, Jimmy Carter, the Americans too were to become more overtly critical of South Africa.

Carter stressed that furthering human rights was a central goal of his foreign policy and American support would be dependent on the degree to which regimes observed such rights. This was not mere rhetoric and Carter appointed Andrew Young, who had been a prominent leader of the American civil rights movement, as the United States ambassador to the United Nations. Young took an active interest in the affairs of southern Africa. He was very critical of the Rhodesia

Front and at one stage went so far as to condone the Cuban military presence in Angola.

The South Africans grew increasingly concerned at these developments, not least because of the arms embargo but also because of their growing fear of Soviet and Cuban military expansion in the region. Hitherto the South Africans had confidently been able to take on any of the frontline states or even all of them simultaneously because of their superiority in conventional forces, but the prospect of having to confront the Soviet Red Army (or Cuban or East German surrogates) was an altogether different proposition. They would not be in a position to replace the loss of main battle tanks or modern combat aircraft because of the UN arms embargo.

In modern warfare air superiority is of vital importance, as was shown during the Falklands conflict in 1982, and is particularly important in southern Africa because of the clear skies, which means that the weather never prevents the use of aircraft. This means that, once air superiority is established, ground forces (especially tanks, armoured personnel carriers and infantry) are extremely vulnerable to air attack. The only military threats that the South African government has to fear are the intervention of one of the major superpowers on the side of one of the frontline states or the escalation of the use of the Cuban combat forces in Angola.

The Fall of Rhodesia

Vorster realized that the Frelimo victory in Mozambique in 1975 meant that the Rhodesian government of Ian Smith was on borrowed time and that inevitably the war would tilt decisively in favour of the guerrillas. Rhodesia's international isolation had to be broken and some form of majority rule agreed with the country's black population. After all, if the South Africans could have their candidate installed as Prime Minister, or at least if a pro-Western regime were to come to power, such as that of Dr Hastings Banda in Malawi, then a further Soviet presence in the area could be countered. The South Africans were already having to contribute to the Rhodesian defence budget as well as lending the support of men and equipment. What was of paramount importance for the South Africans was that a pro-Soviet regime be excluded from power. The northern border would be secure as long as any Rhodesian government did not invite Soviet or Soviet surrogate forces on to its territory nor give assistance to guerrillas of the African National Congress.

Ian Smith was reluctant to introduce any reform but pressure from South Africa in the form of delays in the supply of oil proved to be an effective reminder of how vulnerable Rhodesia was to South African pressure. Smith embarked on a plan to share power with some internal leaders of the black opposition, while excluding the guerrilla groups, ZIPRA and ZANLA, and their leaders Joshua Nkomo and Robert Mugabe. Instead Smith chose to negotiate with Bishop Abel Muzorewa, the Reverend Ndabaningi Sithole and Chief Chirau, whom he perceived as being more pliant. The Rhodesian Front believed that if it had a black government with the key portfolios of Defence and Home Affairs, along with control of the security forces, in white hands, then it would largely be able to carry on as before, simply having black figureheads in government. Once an agreement had been reached and these internal leaders had gone along with it, sanctions would be lifted and external help could be acquired to fight the guerrilla forces and the Western powers could lean on the frontline states to withdraw their support from the guerrillas.

An election was held in 1979, which Bishop Muzorewa duly won but international recognition was not forthcoming. The reason for this was that the political parties representing the guerrilla groups (the Zimbabwean African People's Union (ZAPU) was ZIPRA's political wing, while the Zimbabwean African National Union (ZANU) was ZANLA's political arm) were prevented from participating in the election. The frontline states also refused to recognize the new government, arguing that no real change had taken place and that ZANU and ZAPU were the real representatives of the black Rhodesians. The frontline states ensured that other African states as well as Britain and France would not recognize the new regime. The reluctance to bring about a fundamental transformation in the distribution of power showed the intransigence of the Rhodesia Front government.

For the South Africans, it meant that they had to try again to secure a friendly black government in Rhodesia. The key was Britain and under what terms Britain would recognize a black government in Rhodesia that excluded ZAPU and

ZANU. Although the Conservative Party in opposition initially promised to recognize any Muzorewa government, it soon revised this view once in office after the general election of June 1979. It was clear that not only would the frontline states not recognize this government, but neither would the other states of the British Commonwealth nor Britain's allies in the European Community. For the government of Rhodesia-Zimbabwe, the law and order situation continued to deteriorate and the Rhodesian security forces began to launch attacks deeper and deeper into the countries that harboured ZANLA and ZIPRA guerrillas.

More ominously for both Rhodesia-Zimbabwe and South Africa, the Soviet Union and its Cuban allies began to offer their combat forces to Zambia and Mozambique in order to defend these countries from the Rhodesian security forces. Britain's Foreign Secretary Lord Carrington offered to host a conference in London between the government of Rhodesia-Zimbabwe and the guerrilla organizations of ZAPU and ZANU.

Each party and its supporters hoped for victory from the conference. The British threatened to proceed with the conference even if any of the parties walked out. Britain also needed the backers of each group to make their influence felt at important times. The Zambians and Mozambicans saw their economies crumbling and needed to be rid of the guerrilla forces on their soil; consequently, they were both to tell their protégés in the joint ZANU-ZAPU Patriotic Front that if they were the ones to wreck the conference, they could not expect indefinite support. Likewise, the South Africans needed to exert pressure to keep the Rhodesians at the table.

The South Africans believed that if they could not get Muzorewa, their preferred candidate, elected, they would at least be able to get Nkomo to head a coalition with Muzorewa and the white Rhodesians. Smith was suspicious and told the rest of his delegation and Carrington that Carrington's proposals for a settlement would provide a Mugabe victory. The South Africans thought Smith was bitter and David Smith, General Walls and the rest of the Rhodesian delegation opted to push ahead, hoping that a favourable solution could be reached. The South Africans maintained a large presence in Rhodesia-Zimbabwe up to the elections but swiftly and quietly withdrew following the comprehensive victory of Mugabe and his ZANU (PF) party. Mugabe made statesmanlike reconciliations with his former enemies and kept on General Walls as head of the army and Ken Flower as head of the CIO. He did not allow ANC bases in independent Zimbabwe nor did he permit the stationing of either Russian or Cuban troops on Zimbabwean soil. Mugabe had been supported by the Chinese, while his rival Nkomo had been backed by the Russians and the Cubans. Mugabe was aware that the Cubans had organized a contingency plan for a conventional invasion of Rhodesia in order to place their candidate in power as they had done in Angola.

Total Onslaught

The fall of white Rhodesia meant that the cordon sanitaire around South Africa was almost gone. By 1981 only Namibia remained between South Africa and black-ruled states. Even there, the bush war was absorbing more and more South African resources. Under P.W. Botha, the new security management system that had been introduced by Vorster was finally put into practice. These management structures gave much more power to the military in the decision-making process. Botha had been greatly influenced by his Defence Minister Magnus Malan and the latter was influenced by the writings of French counter-insurgency expert André Beaufre. Beaufre believed that guerrilla wars were attacks on every level of society and involved both internal and external assaults to bring down the target government. In Malan's view, South Africa was under a total onslaught from guerrilla forces inside the country but with external support from the frontline states. The malign hand of the Soviet Union was seen as the paymaster and sponsor of the ANC, the Angolan government, the Cubans and the other Warsaw Pact forces that kept the MPLA in power.

This total onslaught was a combined attack from both the expansionist Soviet Union and its satellites and also from the decadent West, which had lost the will to fight for its own interests. The calls for sanctions against South Africa were part of an economic plot by the Soviet Union and its allies to destabilize the country. Total onslaught also involved the organization of strikes, which were aimed at crippling the country's industry. The assault against South Africa was military, involving both a conventional threat and terrorism, economic and political, in that the African and communist states tried to isolate South Africa from other anti-communist countries. Pro-Soviet front organizations in Western Europe and North America encouraged their governments to condemn South Africa.

The response to total onslaught was total strategy. Total strategy meant that all the nation's resources needed to be mobilized to fight the *rooi gevaar* (red menace). This involved a major build-up of the South African Defence Force (SADF) to increase its strength, numbers and equipment. The government attempted to become self-sufficient in more areas of weapons production and also to circumvent the UN arms embargo.

A number of countries in both the Middle East and Latin America were prepared to sell weapons to the South Africans, although at higher prices than normal. In some cases, this was because of ideological sympathy for South Africa's strong anti-communist policies; in other cases, it was simply to make money.

The South African military was very heavily influenced by the thinking of the Israeli military in its conflicts with the Palestinian Liberation Organization in Lebanon. The Israelis had managed to create a buffer zone in south Lebanon, patrolled by sympathetic Christian militias. The Israelis armed and helped to finance these groups in order to keep the Palestinian guerrillas as far away from their borders as possible. The South Africans, in turn, looked to dissident anti-government forces in the frontline states to perform the same function for them. The repressive policies of the Angolan and Mozambican governments were instrumental in driving people into the arms of UNITA in Angola and the Mozambique National Resistance (MNR or Renamo) in Mozambique, which greatly facilitated the task of the South Africans. In Zimbabwe, the ZANU government was based on the Mashona speakers who constituted 80 per cent of the population, whereas the governments of Angola and Mozambique, like that of South Africa, depended on minority ethnic groups for their support. The South African government was also prepared to mount major military invasions of Angola to attack both SWAPO and ANC bases and to counter Cuban offensives against UNITA. The major South African operations were: Reindeer (1978), Smokeshell (1980), Protea (1981) and Askari (1983).

Although these South African incursions attracted international criticism, the forward strategy of the generals brought its rewards when first Mozambique and then Angola were forced to sign agreements with the South Africans. In 1984 the government of Mozambique signed the Nkomati Accord, in which the Mozambicans formally renounced support for the ANC, while the South Africans withdrew support from Renamo. Renamo, however, expanded its operations in the years after the Nkomati Accord until the Mozambique government was able to secure military assistance from Zimbabwe in order to mount an offensive into the guerrilla strongholds of the Gorongosa Mountains.

The Lusaka Accord of 1984 was intended to settle the conflicts over the South African support for UNITA and Angolan support for SWAPO, but the key implications were the questions of the role of the Cubans in southern Africa and the issue of Namibian independence. These problems remained open until 1988, when a more permanent solution was arranged.

Nkomati and After

At first the Nkomati Accord seemed to reflect a victory for the forward strategy of the generals, as Mozambique and subsequently Angola were forced to the negotiating table and to recognize South Africa's security interests.

It soon became clear, however, that neither the South Africans nor the Frelimo government in Mozambique intended to abide by the Nkomati Accord. ANC guerrillas continued to infiltrate South Africa via the Kruger National Park and the Mozambican border, while the South African government continued to supply Renamo with arms and ammunition. However, attacks by the SADF against Mozambican targets seemed to show duplicity on the part of the South African government, and damaged its international image. Furthermore, these attacks stimulated support for sanctions against South Africa and led to increased military intervention by both Western and Soviet forces. This had the effect of tilting the military balance of power towards the frontline states and away from South Africa.

In 1986 the Soviet Union helped to create an extensive network of anti-aircraft defences in southern Angola, including anti-aircraft radar, over 1500 anti-aircraft guns and over 500 surface-to-air missile batteries. The Soviet Union also sold more advanced Mig-23s to the Angolan air force and provided increased training to both the Angolan air force and army. This meant that because of the inability of the South African air force and arms procurement agency ARMSCOR to replace combat aircraft, the South Africans had severely to restrict their use of air power in southern Angola. No longer could they rule the skies as they had done for most of the 1970s, nor could they use air power in support of ground operations, thus further limiting their military options for intervention. The Cuban government increased the number of Cuban combat troops from 40 000 in 1982 to 60 000 in 1988. Great Britain also sent a small military mission to Zimbabwe and Mozambique to help the Frelimo government fight the anti-communist Renamo guerrillas. Although the British presence was small, it was significant and carried great weight in deterring South African government attempts to destabilize Zimbabwe and Mozambique. This was because Britain was one of the most prominent opponents of sanctions against South Africa and the South African government could not afford to antagonize the British by attacking military targets where British military personnel were stationed.

The increased use of covert action by South African special forces meant that the governments of the frontline states grew better prepared to resist such attacks and from 1988 onwards, a greater number of such covert operations went wrong and a number of South African security personnel ended up as prisoners in Botswana and Zimbabwe. South Africa's economic vulnerability was becoming more obvious. The financial cost of the guerrilla war in Namibia was rising, as was the cost of public expenditure on the defence budget. The cost of replacing expensive items of military equipment continued to grow during the 1980s. The South African navy developed plans to build its own submarines and the South African air force revamped its Mirage aircraft under the name of Cheetah, but the plan to build submarines was abandoned because of the colossal expense and the Cheetah's performance fell well below the standards of the contemporary combat aircraft used by both the NATO and Warsaw Pact forces. If the superpowers were to continue to assist the frontline states, then it was only a matter of time before the superior training of the South African forces would be offset by their superior equipment, especially in vital areas such as air power. Coupled with South Africa's worsening economic position, the governments of first Botha and then de Klerk were obliged to seek a reduction in military expenditure and to explore the options of an accommodation with both their internal and external enemies.

The South Africans were heavily committed in Namibia and were extremely reluctant to leave until they had secured an international agreement that guaranteed the withdrawal of Cuban troops from the country. The South Africans had taken over Namibia, then a German colony, during the First World War and they were subsequently given a mandate to govern it by the League of Nations. However, the League of Nations collapsed with the onset of the Second World War. In 1945 the United Nations (UN) organization was formed, one of its main objectives being the dissolution of the old colonial empires. In the late 1940s there was an intensive debate as to whether or not League of Nations mandates were still valid or whether the UN was to take over responsibility for former mandated territories that had not been granted independence. The International Court of Justice gave an advisory opinion in 1950 that the League of Nations mandates were still valid, thus ruling in South Africa's favour. During the 1950s and 1960s, as more and more peoples in Africa became independent and joined the UN, so they not only criticized South Africa's internal policies of apartheid but also the South African presence in Namibia. In 1960 Ethiopia and Liberia took South Africa to the International Court of Justice, arguing that the General Assembly of the United Nations was legally qualified to carry out the functions which had previously been the responsibility of the League of Nations; this referred to matters relating to the administration of territories which had been entrusted to individual countries under League of Nations mandates. Furthermore, they also argued that the implementation of apartheid policies in Namibia was in violation of the League of Nations mandate. The mandate issue was *ultra vires* until the UN declared the League of Nations mandate system revoked in 1969.

Although the International Court of Justice ruled in South Africa's favour in 1950, the UN passed a series of resolutions condemning the South African presence and eventually, in

1967, the United Nations General Assembly passed a resolution condemning South Africa for not complying with previous resolutions urging self-determination for South-West Africa. Further resolutions followed in 1968, following the trial and sentencing of members of the South-West Africa People's Organization, and these resolutions were echoed by the United Nations Security Council. In March 1969 the United Nations Security Council passed another resolution that recognized the end of the League of Nations mandate system and condemned the South African presence in Namibia as illegal and detrimental to the interests of the population. The UN Security Council in 1970 decided to ask the International Court of Justice for an opinion on the continued South African occupation of Namibia in violation of all UN resolutions. The court's majority opinion, given in 1971, was a further condemnation of the South African presence.

Despite the external challenges to the South African presence in Namibia, the government in Pretoria had its own plans for the future of the country. The South Africans were most concerned to keep the Marxist SWAPO from power. This was likely to be a difficult policy to implement in the long term because SWAPO, originally called the Ovambo People's Organization, were based on the Ovambos, who were the largest ethnic group in Namibia. The South Africans, however, hoped to develop an internal settlement by encouraging an alternative political coalition opposed to SWAPO inside Namibia.

This was the aim of the conference they set up at Turnhalle in Windhoek. A new anti-SWAPO political grouping was formed and became known as the Democratic Turnhalle Alliance (DTA), which included many of the leaders of ethnic groups in Namibia other than the Ovambos. The South Africans initially intended to see the DTA as the government in an independent Namibia. No sooner had the South Africans embarked on this strategy than the UN Security Council passed resolution 435 in 1978, by which they insisted that only UN-supervised elections would be considered legitimate and acceptable to the international community.

The fall of Angola to Marxist forces in 1975 had initially helped SWAPO's guerrilla war but the South African raids into southern Angola and the hostility between the anti-communist guerrillas of UNITA and the Marxist SWAPO meant that SWAPO's military effectiveness was very limited. Yet as time went by, the financial cost of maintaining a large military force in Namibia took its toll on South Africa. Although the South African forces were doing well against the guerrillas, the latter were able to mobilize an increasing number of volunteers. Other factors, too, influenced South Africa to change its policy on Namibia and to come to terms with SWAPO. Securing the withdrawal of Cuban troops from Angola in return for Namibian independence came to be seen as a more important policy objective by the South African government. If this could be accomplished then South Africa's main strategic threat would be removed. Hopes had faded for the DTA which was frequently torn with internal disagreements and clearly was not going to provide any effective alternative government to that of SWAPO. The failure of an internal settlement in Zimbabwe had also discredited the idea of trying to create an alternative to SWAPO. If a SWAPO government in Windhoek were not to have foreign combat forces on its soil, then there was no reason why the government in Pretoria could not come to terms with it.

The United States played a key role in the negotiations for Namibian independence, especially the Secretary of State for African Affairs, Chester Crocker. Both the United States and the Western Contact group, which included Britain, France and West Germany, had an interest in ensuring that an independent Namibia did not become another Soviet satellite state. In 1988 a trilateral agreement was reached between Angola, Cuba and South Africa whereby the UN would supervise elections in which all parties would participate, and SWAPO forces would be allowed to gather at certain points just as the Patriotic Front guerrillas had done in Zimbabwe. Although several incidents threatened this agreement and led to major clashes between SWAPO guerrillas and the SADF, the independence process reached a successful conclusion in 1990 when SWAPO won the country's first free election.

The pre-eminence of the military under P.W. Botha came to an end when F.W. de Klerk became State President. His determination to reach accommodation with his internal political opponents was mirrored by a more conciliatory foreign policy towards the frontline states. The Soviet Union, too, was keen to see an end to conflict in the region. As the

Western countries such as Great Britain, West Germany and the United States pressurized South Africa towards a negotiated settlement, the Soviet Union did likewise with the Angolan government, SWAPO and Cuba. With the steady dismantling of apartheid and the greater participation of blacks in government, South African foreign and defence policies will no longer be fashioned to view so many of its neighbours as the enemy.

The South African Security Apparatus

During the 1980s South Africa possessed the most powerful military machine on the continent of Africa. The South African security forces comprised the following elements: the South African Defence Force (SADF), the South African Police (SAP) and the National Intelligence Service (NIS). The South African Defence Force is subdivided into the South African Army (SAA), the South African Navy (SAN), the South African Air Force (SAAF) and the South African Medical Service.

The largest branch of the SADF is the army. The army is made up of both career soldiers, who are known as the permanent force, and conscripts doing their national service. In 1968 compulsory national service was introduced for all white males and in 1977 this was extended to two years.

Under P. W. Botha's term as Defence Minister, the army underwent an expansion both in terms of manpower and equipment. This build-up of military strength was designed to offset South Africa's growing international isolation and the growth in strength of the anti-colonial guerrilla movements. The Soviet and Cuban intervention in the Angolan civil war and the failure of the Western powers to counter it, heightened South African fears of isolation.

South African defence planners prepared contingencies for fighting both a sustained guerrilla war in Namibia and possibly within South Africa, but also for the possibility of a conventional war against any of the frontline states or a possible combination of the frontline states. In fact such preparations included the probability that Cuban or Warsaw Pact forces might be fighting with the Angolan or Mozambican forces.

This possibility meant that the SADF required to increase their conventional forces, including their main battle tanks and their fleet of armoured personnel carriers. The SADF acquired a number of Centurion tanks from Britain in the 1950s and 1960s. During the 1980s these tanks were improved and redesignated Oliphants. This programme of upgrading and improvements included the use of laser sights, improved communications systems, engines, and armour. However, main battle tanks could not be committed to a conflict unless the South Africans were assured air superiority, because without it their tanks would be exposed to easy attack from the air; as happened so dramatically to the Iraqi tank forces in Kuwait in 1991. The South Africans had to be careful about committing their main battle tanks for two further reasons: first, the weather conditions in southern Africa meant aircraft were very rarely grounded, hence making air superiority essential, and second, the SADF knew that because of the international arms embargo in 1977, it would be almost impossible to obtain replacements for any combat losses that they might suffer.

However, the retention of a substantial force of main battle tanks was an essential insurance against the possibility of a conventional assault by external powers. During the early 1980s the SADF found that the Angolan government's forces made greater use of armour and that the SADF required some form of effective means of resisting tanks and Armoured Personnel Carriers (APCs) without committing the Centurion or Oliphants to battle.

Financial cost was a factor that came to influence defence thinking in countries which maintained combat forces. If a £1000 missile could destroy a £25 million aircraft, then air forces would have to be very careful in their deployment of forces. The loss of tanks, aircraft and warships was becoming extremely expensive by the early 1980s and, consequently, defence experts were seeking ways to be cost efficient. One area where advances were made was in the field of anti-tank and anti-aircraft weapons systems. Advances in anti-tank weaponry meant that substantial damage could be inflicted on tank forces for relatively small amounts of money. Hence resources were concentrated on priority areas of weapons expenditure and procurement in order to obtain the best value for money. Examples of such spending were on the Cactus anti-aircraft weapons system and on the 155 mm G-5 and G-6 self-propelled guns.

One area where the SADF developed a large number of their own items of equipment was in the sphere of Armoured Personnel Carriers and Armoured Fighting Vehicles (AFVs). These were necessary for two reasons. First, the victors in most successful conventional wars not only required air superiority and a powerful force of tanks but also a highly mobile force of mechanized infantry. Therefore the SADF required a large number of APCs to transport infantry behind their tank force for conventional battles.

However, more importantly for the SADF was the requirement of APCs and AFVs for counter-insurgency purposes. In most of the theatres of operations in which the SADF operated, APCs were better suited to the terrain than tanks. For example, this was certainly the case during the long guerrilla war in Namibia and also for the SADF sorties into Angola. Even within South Africa, APCs were of considerable use in combatting unrest in the townships, such as Soweto and Alexandria.

The most important feature of the South African APCs was their resistance to landmines. Landmines could often cripple slow-moving tanks and other forms of tracked vehicles, thus making them vulnerable to either anti-tank weapons or air attack. The Elands and the Ratels made up the majority of the SADF AFVs. The Elands were updated versions of the old British vehicle but were fitted with a number of local specifications.

The South African Army

Unlike the British army, the South African army is not an all-volunteer force. The army took over 70 per cent of the full-time manpower of the SADF and over 50 per cent of the defence budget. For most of the post-1945 period, the defence budget averaged just under 10 per cent of government spending and only increased to just under 16 per cent of public expenditure between 1976 (the Soweto uprising) and 1984 (the uprising in the townships following the introduction of Botha's new constitution). The core of the army is the full-time permanent force, whose upper echelons are almost exclusively Afrikaner. Yet this permanent force often comprises less than 30 per cent of the army manpower.

The white citizens of South Africa faced life-long commitments to the SADF. Military training would often begin at school or in youth groups and once a male had reached the age of eighteen years, he would be obliged to do two years of full-time service with the SADF, although this could be deferred for those who were going to undertake a university degree course.

Once that two years of conscription was completed, the South African soldier could expect to be called on to serve a further twenty-four months' service over the next fourteen years in the Citizen Force. This meant that the average South African male would still have significant military commitments until he was thirty-six years old. Even then he could still be called on to perform twelve days a year until he was fifty-five years old. He would serve a five-year period in the Active Citizen Force Reserve and finally a further period in the Commandos. It should be noted that in South Africa the Commandos were not an élite combat unit but something more akin to the British Home Guard units of the Second World War. The two principal élite combat units were the Parachute Brigade and the Reconnaissance Commandos. The latter unit was similar in both their training and performance capability to the British Special Air Service.

Older members of the SADF could be used for guard duties, while the younger members would be used in the combat zones in Namibia and Angola. This process of militarizing white South African society had several consequences. In the first place it meant that in the mid-1980s the SADF could deploy 150 000 men with a further 700 000 in trained reserves to fall back on. Although this large military machine looked impressive, several qualifications needed to be added to the figures. These numbers represented almost the maximum mobilization of white manpower and were it to be committed to battle, there were no further reserves to be tapped. Second, this force could not afford to take substantial casualties for exactly the same reason. There were not replacements for any significant casualty losses. Third, South Africa could not afford to have this quantity of manpower away from industry for any prolonged period, because the whites made up a substantial proportion of both skilled workers and managers.

There was a further implication for manpower planning for the SADF that followed on from its dependency on the white population. If white manpower resources were being stretched, then other sources had to be considered. There were three options open to the SADF in this regard. First, they could recruit more women into the service. This option would clearly only free a limited number of ancillary roles as white culture would not permit women to be deployed in combat zones as soldiers. Nevertheless, the number of women in the SADF did increase during the 1980s. By 1991 there were around 4000 white women in the SADF.

Second, they could look for foreign mercenaries in order to acquire trained combat forces. In some cases this was done: for example, there were substantial numbers of former members of the British armed forces who went to join the SADF as there were ex-soldiers from Australia, Canada and New Zealand. However, the major foreign intakes in the 1970s and 1980s came from Portuguese and Rhodesians. However, not all of these intakes were successful and, in any case, these were once-off recruits who were fleeing from the new governments in their former homelands. Mercenaries were also of varying quality. Although many would be sound professional service-men, others would be adventurers or those looking to find an outlet for cruelty in a battle zone, where traditional rules of military discipline and restraint might not apply.

Third, they could recruit more blacks to the armed forces. There were a variety of ways that more blacks could be incorporated into the SADF. One method was to increase the number of black volunteers into regular units, another was to create separate black units under white officers. The creating of separate black units raised an additional series of questions. Should they be set up on an ethnic basis or on an integrated basis? Clearly both options contained different sets of prob-lems. The example of Lebanon showed that ethnically-based military units could disintegrate in the event of heightened ethnic conflict and could not be guaranteed to serve a government on an impartial basis. However, in Rhodesia and Mozambique black units served very successfully in the counter-insurgency campaigns.

There was also the possibility of increasing the defence units of the black homelands. However, whilst these units could be useful in maintaining order within the homelands, the homelands created their own political élites with their own interests and agendas. In some cases, homelands forces might be opposed to the ANC but in others they might be sympathetic to it.

Another problem with the militarization of white society was that, inevitably, a certain number of whites will become disillusioned with both the state and the military and will be tempted to evade military service. Draft evasion may be caused by a dislike of being conscripted into the army but it may also be caused by political dislike of the government of the day. Conscription is always an unpopular policy even in times of war and often acts to stimulate domestic opposition to a government. Conscription in Ireland in 1918 helped swing support to the Irish Republican Army in their war against the British government. During the 1960s opposition to conscription in the United States was one of the major factors that fuelled protests against the Vietnam War and the Johnson and Nixon governments. Likewise in South Africa, extensions in the call-up periods for young males increased support for groups opposing not only conscription but also the SADF and the policies of the Vorster and Botha governments.

Between 1970 and 1977 the rate of draft evasion increased from 11 per cent to over 25 per cent of eligible recruits. In many cases, these were students who went abroad for holidays prior to their call-up or after they had completed their university education and they subsequently failed to return to South Africa. Although a number of these men remained in the frontline states, the majority went to Britain, the United States or the Netherlands.

The South African Navy

The South African Navy (SAN) had traditionally been the least Afrikaner branch of the armed forces. Until 1975 the SAN had seen itself as operating in alliance with the Royal Navy and other NATO forces. To this end, Britain had retained the use of the Simonstown naval base until the mid-1970s. The SAN saw its task as the guarding of the Cape route, around which passed most of the oil from the Persian Gulf on its way to Europe and North America.

However, following what many South Africans felt was inadequate Western support during the Angolan civil war in 1975, the SAN was given the revised brief of simply guarding South African coastal waters. Although its headquarters was in Pretoria, the main SAN base was Simonstown in the Cape Province with the main training academy at Saldanha Bay in the Cape Province. The SAN did not have a large fleet. The SAN, like the rest of the SADF, relied on a small force of permanent members and a large number of national servicemen. The use of so many national servicemen was not without its drawbacks. It meant that a large number of regular servicemen were constantly involved in training new recruits and hence not available for action. On the other hand, because of the extensive territorial and citizen force commitments to service for most of their adult life, all arms of the SADF had a large supply of well-trained manpower at its disposal. The offsetting cost of such a military capability was that an important pool of skilled and managerial manpower was taken out of the economy for long and unnecessary periods.

The SAN was divided into four sections: the submarine flotilla, the frigate squadron, the flotilla of Fast Attack Craft (FACs) and Mine Countermeasures vessels. The frigates were more of symbolic value than of practical necessity to a coastal patrol navy. They were expensive to build and maintain, and could be easily destroyed with relatively inexpensive missiles. With the 1977 arms embargo and the increased isolation of South Africa, it was clear that the SAN was not going to obtain replacements for its elderly frigates.

The SAN had three Daphne class submarines, which were purchased from France in the 1970s. A further order was placed for two Agosta class submarines, which, although built, were not delivered because of the United Nations arms embargo. Further rumours abounded in the mid-1980s that the Armscor had obtained the designs for a West German-type 206 submarine and that the hull was to be built on the Rand and subsequently transported to Durban or Richards Bay for completion. The plans for such submarines were abandoned due to costs in the late 1980s.

SOUTH AFRICAN NAVY DAPHNE CLASS SUBMARINES

SAS   Maria van Riebeck
SAS   Emily Hobhouse
SAS   Johanna van der Merwe

The choice of an initial order of two Agosta class submarines was unusual because it would be normal to purchase submarines in orders of three. One submarine going out on patrol, one coming back and one being refitted. It is only by using this method that a navy can guarantee to have one submarine always on alert. For the purposes of a coastal navy, it was difficult to see the need for South Africa to maintain more than a small number of submarines. As it happened, the most regular combat function of the Daphne class submarines was to land Commandos along the coastline of either Mozambique or Angola.

The submarine force is also used to monitor Soviet naval activity in the southern Atlantic and Indian oceans. The Soviet naval presence in these areas has greatly increased since the 1970s.

However, Soviet naval activity can also be watched from the major intelligence and communications centre at Silvermine. Although both the NATO and Warsaw Pact forces monitored each others naval deployments by both satellite and conventional means, the waters of the southern Atlantic provided some unique problems even for the most sophisticated technology. For example, salination levels, influenced by the meeting of the Atlantic and Indian oceans, made the tracking of submarines a particularly difficult task. This was significant in geo-strategic terms because so much of the nuclear weapons, used by NATO and to a lesser extent the Warsaw Pact forces, were submarine launched. Hence the waters off southern Africa were an ideal place for submarines to go in order to escape detection from their opposing monitors. Second, as the 1979 'Vela' incident showed, the waters off the coast of South Africa proved difficult to monitor for another reason. In 1979, American Vela satellites had picked up what analysts believed was the usual recording of the explosion of a nuclear device off the coast of South Africa. The first question that the Americans asked was whether or not the South Africans had exploded a nuclear bomb and if not then what had caused their satellite to register such an explosion? Clearly from the location, the South Africans were the party responsible for the explosion but some debate existed as to whether or not the explosion was a nuclear bomb or some other sort of a device. Second, there was concern as to whether the explosion was solely a South African affair or whether one of the allies, such as Taiwan, Chile or Israel, had also been involved in the testing of new weapons.

Other countries that had small navies but that faced procurement problems were Israel and Taiwan. In the case of both countries, they were unable to spend money on all of the armed services and consequently they had to prioritize the most important areas of expenditure. Both of these countries declined to invest large sums of money in expensive warships but rather spent their naval allocations on Fast Attack Craft. The influence of Israeli thinking was particularly important on South African naval thinking on these matters.

Two major issues faced the SAN during the 1980s with regard to their future maritime role. While South Africa was becoming more isolated from the NATO powers, it developed closer ties with several Latin American countries. Argentina, Chile and Brazil were all governed by authoritarian anti-communist military dictatorships. The navies of these countries shared concern at the growing Soviet naval presence in the southern Atlantic but also faced criticism from Western Europe and North America for their record on abuses of human rights. Faced with criticism from their traditional allies, all these countries contemplated setting up a South Atlantic Treaty Organization (SATO). Such an organization would have been an anti-communist coalition but would have been without the support or involvement of the United States. In any event, the SATO project came to nothing but the South Africans continued to maintain close links with a number of South American governments up until the 1990s.

The 1980s was a difficult time for the SAN, because the army was very much the dominant branch of the SADF and was the most dominant lobbyist for resources and defence procurement. Yet this period also saw some rapid modernizing of SAN in terms of the introduction of new communications and guided-missile weapons systems, such as the Skerpion ship-to-ship missile.

The SAN had 6000 men, including a large contingent of Indian personnel. It was the smallest of the services behind the air force with 11500 and the army with 61000 men. These numbers would all be boosted with the mobilization of the reserves.

The South African Air Force

With 11500 members, the South African Air Force (SAAF) is one of the largest air forces on the continent of Africa. It has

317 combat aircraft and a wide range of transport aeroplanes and helicopters. The SAAF had bought their aircraft from Britain until the 1960s but thereafter had diversified into French and Italian aircraft. Although the SAAF still maintain some elderly Buccaneer fighters, which can deliver a nuclear weapon, the pride of the air force are the Mirage and Cheetah fighters.

The Mirages were acquired in the 1970s and Italian Aeromachiis were built locally under licence as Impalas. An older version of the Mirage was rebuilt and given new Snecma gas engines. This became known as the Cheetah. Although the Cheetah was by no means as fast as the Mig-23 or the more recent NATO or Soviet fighters, the South Africans had developed a number of new weapons systems such as the Kukri air-to-air missile.

The major problem faced by the SAAF has been finding a suitable replacement for her Mirage force while the UN arms embargo remains in force. The SAAF has dominated the skies over southern Africa since 1914. Even during the 1970s, the SADF had total air supremacy over Angola and Mozambique. The SADF used this supremacy to good effect. The SAAF could either carry out a raid against ANC targets by itself, such as the attack on an ANC base in Maputo, Mozambique, in 1983, or it could be used to support ground attacks against ANC or SWAPO bases, such as the attack on the SWAPO base at Kassinga in Angola in 1978.

The SAAF found things became more difficult when the Soviet and Cuban forces deployed an anti-aircraft defensive system across southern Angola. This system included mobile- and radar-controlled anti-aircraft guns and surface-to-air missile batteries. Yet, tactically, the South Africans could evade this system by flying low and along river beds, where the radar had blind spots.

The South African Police

The South African Police (SAP) were in the frontline of the counter-insurgency struggle against the ANC and the PAC and, like the SADF, they are given counter-insurgency training. The SAP has nearly always been short of its target numbers. This is partly because of low pay but also because the numbers in the SAP have risen so dramatically since the 1970s.

THE SOUTH AFRICAN POLICE

Year	Maximum Strength including Reserves
1973	57,700
1979	72,200
1983	82,600
1993	94,000 (estimated target)

It is also worth noting that about half of the SAP are black, a factor which is surprising, considering the enormous extra danger for blacks serving in the force since the early 1980s due to assassinations by the ANC/MK.

The most important arm of the SAP is the Security Branch. This section is responsible for gathering information to arrest members of MK, AZAPO or any other illegal group. The Security Branch is also responsible for enforcement of banning orders. Banning orders are legal punishments aimed at restricting the movements and the activities of those whom the government deem to be subversive. They can be restricted from travelling outside their own town, they can be banned from political activities and from giving interviews to the press. Although such restrictions are of little concern to members of the MK underground, they are of substantial use to the government to harass those engaged in organizing or participating in public-order protests.

The SADF in Comparative Perspective

Despite all the constraints imposed on the SADF, in terms of manpower and access to external supplies of weapons due to the UN arms embargo, it nevertheless remains the most powerful military force in Africa. The SADF remains the best-trained and equipped military machine on the continent, it has the best casualty evacuation facilities of any armed forces on the continent and it is the only nuclear weapons power on the African continent.

The SADF's main military opponent during the 1970s and 1980s was the People's Republic of Angola. The SADF and the Angolan army regularly clashed in southern Angola. The SADF attacked SWAPO and ANC bases in southern Angola and occasionally intervened to help the anti-communist UNITA guerrillas from the combined assaults of the Cuban and the Angolan Marxist minority government. The Angolan government fielded a combined military force of 100000 men with a further 60000 in the reserves. The Angolan government faced a UNITA guerrilla force of 60000 men. The South Africans possessed almost 400 combat aircraft, while the Angolans possessed a mere 191 planes. However, while the South Africans flew and maintained their own aircraft without any outside assistance and in the face of an international ban on supplying their combat aircraft with spare parts, the Angolans were heavily dependent on both the Cubans and East Germans for both the flying of combat missions and the maintenance of their aircraft. Even when the Angolans were given Mig-23 fighters that could outperform the SADF Mirage fighters, the SADF still came out better in air combat because of their superior training and tactics.

The situation between the SADF and the armed forces of Mozambique was even more pronounced. The air force of Mozambique possessed a mere forty-one combat aircraft, which were no match for the SADF Mirage and Cheetah fighters. Mozambique had combined regular forces of just under 70000 men with a further 50000 in reserves. However, these figures looked better on paper than they were in reality. Morale was low, desertions were frequent and the forces were unable to undertake even basic counter-insurgency operations. A large force of Zimbabwean and Tanzanian forces kept the three major railways to the coast open, while the anti-communist Renamo organization kept over 30000 guerrillas under arms against the Mozambican army.

An interesting comparison to consider is the respective defence budgets of South Africa and other African states, especially the frontline states. Although exact figures are not always available, the following statistics illustrate the enormous differences in economic and military might between South Africa and other states on the continent of Africa.

From these figures it is clear that South African military spending is much higher than any other country in sub-Saharan Africa. Its armed forces are more numerous than the combined strength of all of its neighbours put together. It should also be noted that the large 'on paper' strength of a number of African armies is no guarantee of their effectiveness or efficiency in combat. In May 1991 the Ethiopian army collapsed in the face of the guerrilla insurgency in the

DEFENCE BUDGETS OF SOUTH AFRICA AND OTHER AFRICAN STATES

Country	Size of Military Budget (in US dollars)	Year of Figures	Size of Combined Military Forces (inc. reserves)
Angola	$819 million	1987	150,000
Botswana	$ 57 million	1990	5,000
Ethiopia	$471 million	1987	438,000
Kenya	$256 million	1987	30,000
Malawi	$ 22 million	1986	8,500
Morocco	$1.4 billion	1988	293,000
Mozambique	$113 million	1990	120,000
Nigeria	$277 million	1990	107,000
South Africa	$3.9 billion	1990	800,000
Sudan	$956 million	1990	79,000
Tanzania	$223 million	1985	156,000
Zambia	$127 million	1987	16,000
Zimbabwe	$363 million	1989	92,000

provinces of Tigray and Eritrea. The Marxist regime that had governed Ethiopia for so long lacked popular legitimacy among its people and brought them only famine and repression. The Ethiopian government had received large subsidies from the Soviet Union since the mid-1970s and their war machine was only sustained with the aid of a large number of Cuban combat troops and Soviet and Cuban pilots.

With the improvement of relations between the Soviet Union and the West dating from the mid-1980s, Soviet aid to its client states in Africa was swiftly and dramatically reduced. In part, this was because the Russian economy could no longer afford the heavy subsidies to its clients, such as Cuba, Vietnam, Angola and Ethiopia, but also because many Soviet experts had realized that they were pouring scarce resources into lost causes that had no hope of succeeding.

Towards a Regional Peace?

The South African conflict covers not only South Africa but also the other regional conflicts in southern Africa. These have included: the transition from Rhodesia to Zimbabwe; the independence of Namibia; the presence of Cuban combat forces in Angola; the establishment of a legitimate and democratic government in both Angola and Mozambique; and the relationship between South Africa and SADCC in a post-apartheid South Africa.

The South Africans pressurized the Rhodesians to a peaceful settlement of the guerrilla war, while the Mozambican leader Samora Machel did likewise to the guerrilla forces of the Patriotic Front. The independence of Namibia was helped by the Americans, British and Russians all pushing their former allies to the conference table and a peaceful resolution of the conflict. The Namibian conflict also led to a peace accord in the sixteen-year war between UNITA and the MPLA in Angola, while similar peace moves were taking place in Mozambique between the Frelimo government and the anti-communist forces of Renamo.

With the legalization of the ANC and other opposition groups, the South African government no longer faces an external military enemy. Also, with the departure of P.W. Botha as State President, the 'securocrats' have suffered a serious loss of influence in the upper echelons of government. If the peace process between the whites, the ANC and Inkatha continues, then the decline in the influence of the military is likely to continue.

Chapter 4

SOCIAL AND ECONOMIC DEVELOPMENTS

The South African Economy

South Africa is the economic giant of the African continent. It possesses large resources of many key minerals, such as gold, diamonds, uranium, vanadium and coal. Its white population enjoys living standards that compare favourably with Western Europe and North America, but the living standards of the black population are more typical of the rest of Africa. South Africa has an extremely efficient agricultural sector, exporting food to its neighbours, and has the most advanced industrial sector in Africa with a strong base in both the mining and manufacturing sectors. The strong economy is underpinned by a good transport infrastructure of roads, railways and ports, which facilitate the movement of imports and exports.

The South African economy was growing stronger in the 1960s and 1970s but in the early 1980s it began to face a growing number of problems, most of which were caused by the political costs of apartheid. In Western Europe and North America anti-apartheid groups mounted pressure on multinational companies to disinvest from South Africa and also encouraged consumers to boycott South African goods. Banks became less willing to lend money either to the South African government or to private companies.

Several sectors of the economy such as manufacturing and mining required higher numbers of skilled workers than the white sector of the labour market could provide, hence economic growth was retarded by the restrictions placed on black workers. In addition, many more blacks were coming on to the job market and the South African government needed to provide more opportunities for them to prevent economic discontent being translated into political protest.

Recent Economic Trends

Since 1981, the South African economy has faced a series of crises. There were recurring problems with inflation, difficulties with deficits in the balance of payments, high interest

71

rates and severe drought. All these problems contributed to the political turmoil in the country. The blacks faced rising inflation and rising unemployment with increases in the costs of housing and food hitting the urban blacks very severely. These factors caused widespread resentment in the townships and sustained popular support for the anti-government rioting. The white working class also suffered from the inflation and saw a narrowing of the gap between white wages and those of blacks. Hence the growing economic crisis led many of the poorer whites to consider switching their allegiance away from the National Party and towards the Conservative Party.

In 1984 the rand fell from eighty to less than sixty cents against the United States dollar, thus increasing the costs of imports and so further fuelling inflation. An expansion in the money supply had also contributed to inflationary pressures in the mid-1980s. However, it was the looming issue of sanctions that started to cause serious difficulties for the South African economy. Foreign loans both to the South African government and to private companies were only being made on a short-term basis.

In 1985 South Africa faced a major problem in repaying its foreign debts (around $24 billion) on account of its inability to find fresh sources of loans. The government therefore suspended payments of its debts until new arrangements could be made to reschedule them.

Dr Denis Worrall, the South African ambassador to Britain, had threatened that if South Africa were faced with comprehensive economic sanctions, then the government might consider renouncing its foreign debts. Although such a move would have been disastrous for the South African economy, it would equally have been a devastating blow to the international banking system because it would have set a precedent for reneging on debts that other countries might wish to follow. Many Latin American countries such as Mexico and Brazil had much larger foreign debts than South Africa and had they chosen to adopt policies of debt reneging, then this could precipitate a catastrophic crisis for the lending banks of Japan, North America and Western Europe. Despite the rescheduling of South African debts in early 1986, the government was to continue to face problems in acquiring fresh loans because of the pressure on the international bankers from anti-apartheid groups.

Recent Demographic Trends

Ethnic factors have always played a role in both white and black politics. Two groups have dominated the South African white community: the Afrikaners have always been the major group, making up around 60 per cent of the white population, while the English constituted around 35 per cent, with Portuguese, Greeks, Jews, Dutch, Germans and Scandinavians making up the remainder. The English-speaking population has been increased by immigration but this has been offset by emigration.

The Anglo-Boer Wars reflected the struggle for power between the English-speakers and the Afrikaners. However, since the Afrikaners had always been more numerous and traditionally had larger families than the English-speakers, they were assured of their dominant position in the electorate. In the aftermath of the Anglo-Boer War, the Afrikaners divided their votes between the South Africa Party and the National Party. From 1948 onwards, the majority of Afrikaners backed the National Party, thus ensuring its long tenure in office. But as the social structure of the Afrikaners changed and more of them became affluent, they again showed signs of significant divisions in the 1980s. With growing pressure from both domestic and international sources, an increasing number of Afrikaners began to change their traditional allegiance from the National Party to the Conservative Party. Since its victory in the 1948 election, demographic and ethnic factors had always played a role in the calculations of the National Party when it contemplated political and constitutional reform.

In 1980 the population was made up of 16 per cent whites (4.5 million) and 73 per cent blacks (21 million) but according to population projections, by the year 2000, the blacks would have increased at a much faster rate than the whites. If the blacks outnumbered the whites by 5:1 in 1980, by 2000 the proportion was 6:1, by 2020 9:1 and by 2040 17:1.

This meant that although the gap between whites and blacks was not excessive in 1980, it was likely to grow substantially and the whites were likely to bargain from an ever weaker position. The other important consequence that followed on from the demographic projections was the need to generate more jobs in the economy to take account of the growing number of blacks entering the labour market.

In particular, the economy required more skilled labour at a time when the traditional source of skilled manpower, the white working class, was declining as a percentage of the labour force. This obliged employers to turn to the black population as a fresh labour source.

However, the employers realized that it was not simply a case of hiring more blacks to do the jobs of whites but rather a case of more training for blacks at every level. In the past, white governments had spent significantly less on black education than on white schools and universities. H. F. Verwoerd, who had been Prime Minister from 1958 to 1966, had argued that the Bantu (black) should only be educated to a level where he could find menial work as the servant of the white man and not be given ideas that might encourage him to aspire to the lifestyles of the white community. National Party policy on education was slow to free itself from these educational policies of apartheid. By the 1980s, Verwoerd's racist ideas of Bantu education were doomed for ever. The government was committed to narrowing the gap in expenditure between the different ethnic groups. In 1960 black enrolment in secondary education was around 54 600 pupils, but by 1985 it was around 1 200 000 pupils.

In 1980 the government appointed the de Lange Committee to look into education in South Africa. The committee reported in 1981 and recommended that the government should give priority to increasing the resources given to black education and in particular to improving the standard of black teachers. Secondly, the report called for the introduction of nine years' free and compulsory education for all children.

Yet even by the mid-1980s, educational expenditure for blacks was only 10 per cent of that spent on white children and pupil-teacher ratios were 50 per cent higher in black schools than in white institutions. Some progress was made in the tertiary sector, where the English universities such as Cape Town and the Witwatersrand admitted a growing number of black students in order to break down segregated education.

The blacks had the additional problem that they were often taught in their tribal vernacular or in Afrikaans rather than English, which was their preferred choice. One aspect of educational apartheid had been to try and keep the African community away from the liberal English culture either by trying to keep the blacks speaking their tribal languages or by forcing them to adopt the Afrikaans language and culture. The black opposition groups, such as the ANC, repeatedly stated their hostility to Afrikaans and maintained that the main language that united the people of South Africa was English. It was common practice in most African states to continue to use the language of the former European imperial power as a unifying factor rather than permit one tribal language to be used as a national language lest it alienate those from other tribes.

The Black, Asian and Coloured Population

Under the Population Registration Act of 1950, all South Africans were to be classified as one of the following: white, coloured, Indian or black. This categorization was not voluntary but was assigned by the white-controlled authorities. The coloured population are often referred to as the Cape coloured as over 90 per cent of them are resident in the Cape province. The classification of coloured covers a number of racial categories ranging from people who are slightly darker than Caucasian to those who are slightly lighter than Negro. Coloured includes those who are of mixed race, that is to say descended from unions of white male settlers and African women. This classification also includes the descendants of the Muslim Malays.

The coloured population comprises around 9 per cent of the total South African population. They were traditionally closer to the Boers than the English and would have spoken Afrikaans as a first language. However, as with most of the black population, the coloureds saw Afrikaans as a language of oppression, especially after the National Party removed the Cape coloured from the franchise in 1956, and consequently now shared the view that English should be the unifying language in a future non-racial South Africa. Eighty-seven per cent of the coloured population belong to Christian Churches, with the largest group (26 per cent) belonging to the Nederduitse Gereformeerde (Dutch Reformed) Mission Church. The majority of the coloured population live in urban areas, particularly in Cape province where the National government had intended to institute a preferential policy of employing coloured labour.

The Indian community in South Africa comprises 3 per cent

75

of the total population and is almost totally resident in Natal. Its people are 70 per cent Hindu, 20 per cent Muslim, most of the remainder belonging to Christian denominations. Most of the Indians were brought to South Africa as labourers in the nineteenth century and their origins are scattered throughout the subcontinent. This can be seen from the variety of dialects and languages that they use at home. Residence restrictions were imposed on the Indian community outside Natal and the Afrikaner-dominated Orange Free State actually prohibited Indian immigration. The Indians have traditionally enjoyed better educational facilities and standards than the coloureds who in turn enjoy superior facilities than the blacks.

Like the coloured community, the Indians have a high birth rate and although both groups have increased numerically, their percentage of the overall population has remained static since 1910.

The blacks are the largest ethnic group in South Africa comprising 73 per cent of the total population. However, the blacks are not a homogeneous group and are subdivided by language into nine major units:

THE BLACK POPULATION

Group	Percentage of Population	Numbers (m)	Homeland
Zulu	20	5.5	KwaZulu
Xhosa	18	5.2	Transkei & Ciskei
Sotho	13	4.3	Lebowa / QwaQwa
Tswana	9	2.1	Bophuthatswana
Tsonga / Shangaans	3	0.9	Gazankulu
Ndebele	2	0.7	KwaNdebele
Swazi	2	0.7	Kangwane
Venda	2	0.5	Venda

Although the National Party had intended to make all blacks become citizens of their homelands, thus denying them South African citizenship, most blacks resided outside their homelands. Under Vorster and Botha there was a concerted policy of removing blacks from urban areas in order to keep the cities white. This policy caused immense suffering to the black and coloured population: according to official government statistics, over 3.5 million people were forcibly moved from their homes under the apartheid resettlement policies in the years between 1960 and 1982.

In a further attempt to reinforce the removal of blacks and coloureds from white areas and to breathe life into the homelands policy, the National government introduced a programme of economic decentralization with selected economic growth points that bordered the homelands. Although such a policy seemed to offer the prospect of the homelands becoming more economically self-sufficient, the centripetal pull of the South African economy nonetheless attracted more and more blacks into the white heartland areas and away from their homelands.

An alternative form of development was tried for Bophuthatswana. This homeland was nicknamed a casinostan because of its reliance on casinos and tourism as a source of income. One of the main attractions of Bophuthatswana is Sun City, the Las Vegas of southern Africa, which became a beneficiary for South African holiday-makers as Mozambique lost its appeal under the Marxist Frelimo regime.

The Mining Sector

Although diamonds were discovered in the 1860s, it was the discovery of gold on the Witwatersrand in 1886 that brought the big influx of *uitlanders* (foreigners) and, in particular, the British into the Boer republics in large numbers. Economic development was also stimulated by the growth of the railways linking the goldfields to the ports of Lourenço Marques in Mozambique, Durban in Natal and overland to Cape Town in the south-west.

The mining houses eventually came to be dominated by the Anglo-American Corporation and De Beers Consolidated Mines. The Anglo-American Corporation has been dominated by the Oppenheimer family for most of its existence. Ernest and Louis Oppenheimer were the driving force in the company for many years, up to 1945, when Ernest's son, Harry, became the dominant figure until his retirement in 1983. Even up to the year of his death, in 1957, Ernest Oppenheimer remained a dynamic figure in the mining community and he continued to look to develop new mines. One of these was Western Deep, which descends to almost 3800 metres. It took considerable financial investment and the

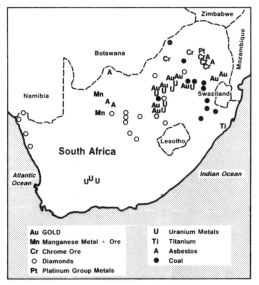

Figure 3   South Africa's Minerals

application of new technology to develop this mine, as there was not only the problem of depth but also of water underground, which added to the hazards for the miners. However, Western Deep was to prove an astute investment with a continuous high output of gold and a life expectancy extending into the middle of the twenty-first century. Anglo-American also own the biggest goldmine in the world, Free State Geduld (also known as FreeGold) which, along with the President Steyn, President Brand, Western Holdings, Vaal Reefs and Western Deep, account for over 50 per cent of Anglo-American gold production.

Harry Oppenheimer's major contribution to the company's growth was his desire to diversify into other areas. His decision involved both extending mining operations into the rest of the world's goldfields and expanding investment into other areas besides mining. The Anglo-American Corporation expanded its mining operations into Rhodesia (now Zimbabwe), Mozambique, Botswana, Namibia, Angola, Zambia, Kenya, the United States, Canada, Brazil and Malaysia. The corporation diversified into many other areas, including: the mining of tin and uranium, banking, investment, breweries, the production of mining equipment, diamonds, oil, platinum, chemicals, coal and property development. Many of these interests are held through Anglo-American holding companies, such as Charter Consolidated and the Minerals and Resources Corporation (Minorco). Although Gavin Relly was to succeed Harry Oppenheimer as chairman of Anglo-American, members of the Oppenheimer family, such as Harry's son Nicholas, still occupy positions of power and influence within the organization.

The Oppenheimers had been longstanding supporters of the liberal opposition in South Africa. They gave assistance to both the United Party and the Progressives and, in particular, had helped to support Mrs Suzman of the Progressive Party, while she remained their sole member in the House of Assembly. Harry Oppenheimer had been a member of parliament in the 1940s and had spent a substantial amount of his money supporting the United Party against D.F. Malan and the Nationalists.

The Anglo-American Corporation had endured cool relations with the Nationalists since Smuts had used the military to break the strike on the Rand in the 1920s. The Nationalists had sided with the white workers against both the mine-owners and the use of black labour. The Nationalists had maintained a strong interest in upholding job reservation for white workers in the mining industry in order to raise their living standards against the threat of competition from the blacks.

After 1948, the National Party was very keen to reward its supporters among the white working class and used the apartheid legislation in order to discriminate further against blacks. Cheap black labour initially helped the profitability of Anglo-American mining operations but as the need for greater amounts of skilled labour became more intense, the labour migration system and job reservation for whites became a major obstacle to economic growth for the corporation.

Relations between the National Party and Anglo-American remained cool during the years of the Verwoerd and Vorster premierships but P.W. Botha made a determined effort to improve relations with big business. The first sign of this new approach from the National Party came in 1979, at the Carlton Hotel in Johannesburg, when Botha outlined the importance of the business community in his scheme for economic decentralization and its importance in his response to the total onslaught that he believed endangered South Africa. Although the business community was initially sympathetic to Botha's reforms, for many these reforms were too slow in coming and only grudgingly implemented. There was particular disappointment over Botha's Rubicon speech in 1985, which both the business community and international opinion had hoped would mark a radical speed-up in the ending of apartheid. As the 1980s continued, and it seemed that Botha was unable to go any further in the direction of reform, Gavin Relly and other businessmen and academics set out to open up their own discussions with the exiled leadership of the African National Congress.

Gold has been the dominant factor in the South African economy. In many countries in the world, the private trading of gold was forbidden; the international exchange of gold was regulated at $35 an ounce and gold continued to be artificially held down to this price until 1968. However, the American dollar came under intense pressure in 1968, due to a number of factors including the Vietnam War, and the United States was obliged to sell a large proportion of its gold reserves in order to protect the value of the dollar. For two weeks the gold market remained closed but once it reopened, the rules governing trade in gold had been changed. Although the official rates of exchange between banks were to remain the same, the market was allowed to decide the price of gold for other transactions, and consequently the price of gold rose steadily for the next twelve years.

Between 1970 and 1975 gold prices varied between $100 and $200 an ounce, but in the late 1970s gold prices climbed steadily, from an average price of $193 in 1978 to an average price of $305 in 1979, eventually peaking in 1980 at $850 an ounce. However, although gold was to retain an average price in excess of $300 an ounce, thereafter, it was not to return to its 1980 price again.

De Beers, Diamonds and the Uranium Industry

The Anglo-American Corporation began as a gold-mining company and, over time, became the most important gold producer in South Africa. However, it also had interests in diamonds, and during the 1920s Anglo-American expanded further into the diamond industry by buying out its major rival, De Beers Consolidated Mines. Anglo-American was to become the major force in the South African diamond industry and subsequently the most important power in the international diamond industry.

Ernest Oppenheimer had inherited an interest in diamonds from the Dunkelsbuhler company (the forerunner of the Anglo-American Corporation), and when Anglo-American acquired Consolidated Diamond Mines in 1919, his diamond holdings increased. The diamond industry did not prosper during the 1920s and consequently the traditional diamond-mining companies lacked the capital to expand. Anglo-American, on the other hand, with its emphasis on gold, did have the resources to expand, and under Oppenheimer it started to acquire new diamond mines in South-West Africa and West Africa.

The diamond companies operated a syndicate in order to monitor production and marketing. As the Anglo-American Corporation increased its diamond holdings, so it increased its influence within the diamond syndicate. Following intense divisions within the syndicate, Anglo-American withdrew in order to form its own syndicate. The old syndicate fell apart and gradually the other diamond producers joined the Anglo-American cartel. More significantly, in 1927, Anglo-American made a bid to take over De Beers, but although the bid failed a further attempt in 1929 was successful and Ernest Oppenheimer was made chairman of De Beers.

During the 1930s the Anglo-American Corporation slowed down the production of diamonds and systematically stockpiled them, in order to force up prices. De Beers then established its Central Selling Organization (CSO), which became an international cartel for the purchase and marketing of diamonds. Over 80 per cent of all the world's diamonds marketed are sold through the CSO. As many southern and central African countries are dependent on one or two mineral exports for most of their foreign currency earnings, it is important for them to get the maximum value for their primary exports. De Beers has managed to obtain consistently high prices for its clients and to avoid the sort of price collapses that have damaged other economies dependent on primary exports. For instance, the fall of the price of tin did enormous damage to the Bolivian economy in the 1970s and the Zambian economy faced a severe crisis following the collapse of the price of copper in the 1980s. Although strident opponents of the South

African government, many Marxist countries, such as the Soviet Union and Angola, were prepared to deal with the CSO.

De Beers owned one of the largest diamond mines in the world at Oranjemund in Namibia, which provided around 16 per cent of De Beers' profits for most of the 1980s. Accordingly, Consolidated Diamond Mines (a De Beers and ultimately an Anglo-American subsidiary) moved its head office to Windhoek, the Namibian capital, in 1977.

Its near global monopoly in the diamond trade meant that De Beers inevitably fell foul of anti-trust legislation in the United States but, despite repeated attempts to prosecute the company, it managed to evade serious inconvenience. The fall in world demand for diamonds in the mid-1980s forced De Beers to hold back on the supply of diamonds once again, just as it had done during the 1930s. As long as De Beers could afford to buy up new diamonds, then it could restrict supply until such time as world demand improved.

The post-1945 period saw the enormous growth of the uranium industry. This growth could be explained by two factors: first, the development of nuclear weapons; and second the use of nuclear power for civil energy purposes. Nuclear weapons required one of two types of fissile material, uranium 235 or plutonium 239. Plutonium is a product obtained from reprocessing spent fuel from a nuclear reactor. The arms race between the forces of the North Atlantic Treaty Organization (NATO) and the Soviet Union and her Warsaw Pact allies led to a growth in the demand for South African uranium in the 1950s.

In the 1960s advances in new technology enabled nuclear power to be used for the commercial generation of electricity and a number of countries, which lacked indigenous sources of coal, natural gas and oil, began to explore the options for the exploitation of nuclear power. Western Europe faced a series of energy problems in the 1970s which increased their willingness to invest in nuclear power programmes. In 1973, as a result of the war between Israel and her Arab neighbours, the main Arab oil-exporting countries threatened to deny oil to any Western European state that might supply arms to Israel. Second, the Organization of Petroleum Exporting Countries (OPEC) quadrupled oil prices, which meant that energy and transport costs automatically increased, and this in turn contributed significantly to inflation in countries that were dependent on cheap imported oil.

France, Belgium and the Netherlands were particularly vulnerable to the interruption of their oil supplies while both the French and the British had the problem of their coal industries becoming ever less competitive in international markets. For France a civil nuclear power programme became a necessity, but it obtained most of its uranium from its former colonies in West Africa, such as Gabon, rather than from South Africa.

In South Africa uranium is obtained as a by-product of gold-mining but in Namibia uranium is mined in its own right. Here, the Rossing mine provides a large quantity but a low quality of uranium. Although South Africa has sizeable reserves of uranium, these are small compared to those of Canada and Australia. However, taken together, South Africa and Namibia, which was under South African control until 1990, accounted for around 22 per cent of all the world's uranium production. The main company engaged in uranium production in South Africa is the Nuclear Fuels Corporation, in which the Anglo-American Corporation has a controlling interest. The Rossing mine in Namibia is controlled by the Rio Tinto Zinc Corporation although it does have a number of British, French, West German and South African partners.

Since the 1950s, one of the central aims of the United States foreign policy has been to restrict the export of nuclear technology that might enable other states to develop nuclear weapons. This non-proliferation policy required the United States to come to an arrangement with both the Soviet Union and the other states that produced uranium and this led to the creation of the International Atomic Energy Association (IAEA) in 1957.

As the international trade in uranium grew during the 1960s, it became harder for the Americans and the Russians to monitor, so in order to rectify this situation they drew up the Non-Proliferation Treaty in 1968, which tried to ensure much tighter safeguards on the inspection of nuclear installations in countries that possessed civil but not military facilities. The intended impact of this treaty was to bind any states that required access to American or Soviet uranium enrichment technology to the full rigours of the IAEA inspection process but also to get them to agree to forego the possession of nuclear weapons.

During the 1970s and 1980s a number of states showed a growing interest in the acquisition of nuclear weapons. These included Argentina and Brazil in Latin America, Israel, Libya and Iraq in the Middle East, India and South Africa. Their motivations for wanting to become a nuclear weapons power were varied. In some cases, such as Israel and India, they were concerned about their inability to deal with conventional assaults from their hostile neighbours, Israel with Egypt, Jordan, Syria and Iraq, and India with China following their border war in the early 1960s.

Both the Americans and the Russians were concerned at these developments for differing reasons. The Americans did not wish to see states that might have conflicting interests with some of their allies acquiring nuclear weapons, while the Russians feared that states with traditional disputes with them might gain access to nuclear weapons in some future conflict. In any event, states that acquired nuclear weapons had the capability to endanger international stability, and this was something which both superpowers wished to prevent.

In accordance with American and Soviet concerns over nuclear proliferation, both the Australians and the Canadians (two of the largest uranium exporters) tightened their restrictions on the exports of uranium. This move was also inconvenient to Western European states such as Britain, France and West Germany because, although all of these states required uranium for peaceful purposes, both the British and the French did require some supplies for their own nuclear weapons programmes. As a result, access to South African uranium assumed increased importance, given the growing difficulties in acquiring uranium from other sources.

The South Africans had been developing their own nuclear programme since the 1940s. They had built three nuclear reactors: Pelindaba, Pelindaba-Zero and Valindaba, the latter built in the 1970s. The South African government established the Uranium Enrichment Corporation (UCOR) in order to expand the development of nuclear technology. During the 1960s and 1970s demands for energy, and in particular electricity, increased. As South Africa was so dependent on imported oil and as oil prices rose so dramatically after 1973, the South African government sought to make more use of nuclear power for electricity generation. Although the Electricity Supply Commission (ESCOM) had a number of coal-burning generators, the South African government wished to use coal stocks for other purposes. First, coal was an important export and earned vital foreign currency, and second, coal was vital to the Sasol project. On account of South Africa's need to import its oil, scientists had developed a process for extracting oil from coal. The first of these plants was built at Sasolberg, the second and third plants at Secunda. The Sasol plants have produced between 35 per cent and 50 per cent of South African liquid-fuel requirements since the mid-1980s.

South Africa's international isolation after 1976 meant that it had become harder to obtain nuclear technology for civil purposes lest such technology have possible military application, which would breach the United Nations arms embargo of 1977. Although companies in Western Europe and North America became reluctant to export technology or equipment to South Africa, two nuclear generating power stations were built and were connected to the electricity grid by 1985. These stations, Koeberg I and Koeberg II, were situated in the Cape province and by 1990 were supplying about 10 per cent of South African electricity needs.

ESCOM had a generating capacity of over 25 000 megawatts (MW) in 1985 with a projection for over 35 000 MW in 1995. Despite its economic difficulties in the 1980s, projections of South Africa's energy requirements are expected to rise sharply in the 1990s and the early twenty-first century in line with demographic increase. South Africa's energy consumption is much higher than any of the other countries on the African continent and this is due not only to the higher levels of education and industrialization in South Africa but also because the planning and development of energy needs have been more far-sighted. South Africa's Atomic Energy Board (renamed the Nuclear Development Corporation in 1982) was set up in the 1940s and has had some extremely dynamic and capable presidents, such as Dr A. J. Roux and more recently Dr W. de Villers.

The Manufacturing Sector

The manufacturing sector of the South African economy has benefited the least from apartheid because the costs of petty apartheid have been higher than the advantages of cheap labour that accrued from apartheid labour policies. Manufacturing industries require an educated and stable workforce, not alternating rotas of unskilled migrant workers. The effects of petty apartheid were needlessly to duplicate facilities, while job reservation not only meant excessive wages to white workers but also a major shortage of skilled workers because the colour bar prevented blacks from being trained for skilled work. Such an arrangement clearly had benefits for the lower echelons of the white labour force.

In the 1980s manufacturing industry also grew increasingly concerned about the political instability in the country and this led it into conflict with the Nationalist government in a number of areas. The government's policy of trying to develop growth points in the homelands in order to keep blacks away from the white metropolitan areas not only worked against the needs of manufacturing industry, but required immense subsidies from it. Very often, too, the management in manufacturing industry wanted to raise wages for blacks to help ameliorate their living conditions, to end the colour bar on jobs and to reduce the difference in wages between black and white workers.

In addition to these measures, many leading businessmen wanted to reduce the differences in government expenditure on education in order to improve the standard of black education. The employers also hoped that it would be possible to recognize black trade unions and bring them into the system. However, many of these policies led the employers in the manufacturing sector into conflict with the policies of the Botha government. Equally, many white businessmen were afraid of the radical anti-capitalist rhetoric of both the ANC and the Black Consciousness Movement and they were concerned that a change in the political order might also mean a change in the economic order from a capitalist economic system to a communist command economy. A number of prominent businessmen therefore began to have separate discussions with the ANC to seek clarifications on their economic policies. On account of its long association with the South African Communist Party, the ANC's economic programme had a pronounced orientation towards nationalization, central controls and planning. However, other governments in southern Africa, such as Angola and Mozambique, that had adopted Marxist policies soon found that the implementation of such programmes caused their economies to collapse.

The disastrous experience of Marxist economic policy in his own country led Samora Machel, the Mozambican president, to advise Robert Mugabe, the Prime Minister (and later President) of Zimbabwe, to adopt a pragmatic approach to economic affairs. Many in the white business community hoped that regular contacts with the ANC would also cause it to moderate its militant rhetoric and endorse the free enterprise system.

In the early 1980s growing sections of the Afrikaner élite urged the National government to ease restrictions on black businesses in South Africa. The reason for this was that apartheid laws had made it very difficult for black traders to build up their own businesses and consequently meant that few blacks had a stake in the capitalist system. It was again hoped that by allowing blacks to make profits and build up their own businesses they would develop a vested interest in the free enterprise system and hence an interest in defending it.

The central problem for blacks was that under apartheid laws they were considered as guest workers in white areas and were subject to strict laws governing their movements. In addition, they also faced intense difficulty in finding accommodation because the government would restrict the number of houses built in areas designated for blacks, thus creating a permanent housing shortage and leaving the existing black urban areas overcrowded. Blacks who were able to live in the urban areas with their families had what was known as Section 10 rights and successive National governments endeavoured to make sure that as few blacks as possible had them.

Inevitably, the black urban areas such as Soweto became breeding grounds for anti-government resentment and any attempt to give legitimacy to urban self-government for the black areas was doomed to failure. Gangsters, known as *totsis*, often terrorized the local inhabitants and even the ANC was unable to control these elements.

South African manufacturing industry expanded between the two world wars although it did suffer as a result of the world recession after 1929. The implementation of the apartheid laws in the 1940s further added to the costs of South African industry. Even in the 1960s South Africa still imported more manufactured goods than it exported. The South Africans were able to use their surplus from the exports of minerals and agriculture to pay for these imports. The huge distances between urban areas and the lack of provision of public transport accounted for a large domestic automobile market. American firms such as Ford, German firms such as BMW and Japanese companies such as Datsun and Toyota moved into South Africa in order to exploit this market.

South Africa's mining and manufacturing sectors are backed up by the most efficient transport infrastructure on the African continent. The country is served by six major ports divided between the Atlantic and the Indian Oceans. Cape Town and Saldanha Bay are on the Atlantic coast, while East London, Port Elizabeth, Durban and Richard's Bay are on the Indian Ocean coast. These ports serve not only South Africa but also a number of the states on South Africa's borders: in part this was due to the pattern of industrialization and European settlement but is also explained by other factors.

During the guerrilla war in Rhodesia, much of Zambia's copper exports as well as all of Rhodesia's agricultural and mineral exports passed through South African ports. Following a conflict between Ian Smith, the Prime Minister of Rhodesia, and Dr Kenneth Kaunda, the President of Zambia, the Rhodesians closed their borders to Zambian rail traffic bound for the Indian Ocean ports of either Lourenço Marques (Maputo) in Mozambique or Durban in South Africa. Before the collapse of the Portuguese African empire, port facilities in Angola were not so swift or efficient as those in South Africa. After Angolan independence, the anti-communist guerrillas of UNITA frequently closed the Benguela railway in southern Angola, while in Mozambique, Renamo guerrillas closed the railway lines to Maputo, Beira and Ncala. In any case, the capacity of these ports to handle cargo greatly decreased after several years of chronic economic mismanagement by the Marxist Frelimo government.

Once the Rhodesian conflict had ended with the triumph of the ZANU (PF) party of Robert Mugabe, the new government of Zimbabwe found that it had many ties of economic dependence on South Africa. In addition to needing port facilities for both imports and exports, the government of Zimbabwe also needed to lease a substantial amount of engines and rolling stock for its own railways.

Most of South Africa's imports and exports were handled by the Indian Ocean ports, which were nearer to the mining and industrial heartland of Pretoria, Witwatersrand and

Vereeniging (the PWV triangle). The Atlantic ports, however, did retain importance because of their military significance. The naval base of Simonstown was the main headquarters for the South African navy and Britain's navy retained facilities there until 1975. The South African naval academy was at Saldanha Bay in the Cape province as was the huge intelligence and communications centre at Silvermine, which also retained provision for NATO members.

The Agricultural Sector

The white farmers had differing interests in the policies of apartheid. Some pieces of discriminatory legislation, such as the 1913 Land Act, effectively got rid of black tenant farmers as competitors to the whites. This act led to many blacks being forced into overcrowded reserves on which they could not possibly make a living. This meant that they would have to seek work either on white farms or in white industry, but in either case they would be a source of cheap labour.

Other white farmers found that it was difficult to get black labourers when they had to compete with the wage rates being offered by manufacturing industry. Therefore they wanted very strict controls on the movement of black labour so that it would be extremely difficult for urban employers to give blacks work. Yet, as the 1980s progressed, there was less opposition from the white farming community to government efforts to develop black agriculture and farming. The growing black population and the growing urban population in South Africa meant that unless food production were to increase, there was a danger that South Africa might have to import food.

Even within the farming community there were different views on the outcome of their economic problems. Some of the larger farmers, who had the benefits of scale on their side, were able to expand, but they tended to be based in Natal, whereas the smaller farmers, particularly those in the Transvaal and the Orange Free State, found themselves more vulnerable to recession. Throughout the 1980s more and more small farmers found themselves with larger debts and so they were forced to move away from the land and towards the cities.

This tendency caused great concern to both the political and military élite in South Africa. Both élites were worried about the whites abandoning large areas of land because they were concerned that without a white presence it would only be a matter of time before guerrilla infiltration would occur.

During the 1980s the South African agricultural sector faced growing problems because of drought. Farmers were confronted with mounting debts (over one billion rand in 1985) and pressed for government intervention to help them. However, the National government was under pressure on many fronts and found it ever more difficult to give handouts to its own supporters when the blacks were so much worse off. The South Africans were able to export a number of crops such as maize (to the value in excess of one billion rand per year), fruit and wheat although their costs were high. They also enjoyed a reputation for exporting good tobacco and wine. Wine production had a long tradition in the Cape province and was particularly associated with the Huguenots, who had settled there as refugees from France in the seventeenth century.

South Africa was one of the few agricultural success stories of Africa and was able to export food to some of its less successful neighbours. Efficient farming techniques had facilitated food production and careful breeding of livestock along with vigorous policies of pest control meant that South Africa avoided many of the problems of her northern neighbours.

The Sanctions Debate

In the 1980s there were growing calls by opponents of the South African government both inside and outside the country for the international community to implement sanctions as a means to bring about an end to the policies of apartheid. Sanctions were felt to be a middle way between war and inaction, although the previous use of sanctions as an instrument of policy in international relations had not been very successful. In the 1930s sanctions were ineffective as weapons to stop the aggressive foreign policies of fascist Italy and imperial Japan. In the 1960s the British government sought the introduction of sanctions by the United Nations against the government of Rhodesia for its unilateral declaration of independence.

The Rhodesian declaration of independence was made in order to preserve white minority rule in what was formerly the

British colony of Southern Rhodesia. The British even sent naval forces to the coast of Portuguese Mozambique in order to prevent the delivery of oil and other specified items. The sanctions were not a success because the government of South Africa and the Portuguese colonial authorities turned a blind eye to the breaking of such sanctions.

The main supporters of sanctions against South Africa were the frontline states and the ANC and their support groups inside and outside South Africa. The frontline states were in a difficult position, on the one hand, since if comprehensive economic sanctions were implemented against South Africa, they would suffer too. On the other hand, if sanctions were successful and brought about an end to apartheid, many among the frontline states hoped that this would mean an end to external support for groups such as UNITA and Renamo, who were fighting the Angolan and Mozambican governments.

A number of supporters of sanctions among the frontline states hoped that if they were to suffer disruption as a result of sanctions the Western countries would make good the damage with generous donations of aid, equipment and low-interest loans. Some of the more vocal advocates of sanctions were those states who would be the least affected by them.

Assessing the wishes of the blacks inside South Africa was also difficult: some groups such as Inkatha opposed sanctions, as did the white liberal opposition, but others such as the ANC strongly supported them. The reasons for the differences among blacks depended on their perceptions about the viability of peaceful change in South Africa. The ANC's position prior to the release of Nelson Mandela was predicated on the principle that even if sanctions would not bring down the National government in Pretoria, they would at least inflict substantial economic misery, making any programme of reforms that did not include the ANC difficult to implement. Among members of the more militaristic and Marxist wing of the ANC was a belief that it would be better to inherit South Africa as a ruin as long as they achieved total control. This view was echoed among many of the right-wing whites, who were quite happy to see sanctions implemented because they believed that it would make a middle path of reform impossible to sell to the white community. In other words, they wanted to see a polarization within the white community in order to prevent the National Party moving away from apartheid.

In 1991 the ANC remained divided about the future of sanctions. It seemed that the leadership, such as Mandela and Tambo, were more flexible on the issue than many of the rank and file members of the organization. However, sanctions have remained one of the cards that the ANC can still wield against the National Party in their negotiations for an ending of apartheid. Clearly one of the signs that a future constitutional arrangement in South Africa had legitimacy would be that the ANC and its supporters would endorse the ending of sanctions.

The case in favour of sanctions was based on the following argument. The objectives were to force the white minority government to hand over political power to a government that represented the majority of all South Africa's citizens. Comprehensive economic sanctions were intended to destroy South Africa's economy to such a point that the white minority government and the white population would find the cost of opposing such a demand so high that they could no longer resist it. Linked to this aim was a subsidiary goal of steadily reducing the military capability of the whites, whether this involved white repression of blacks inside South Africa or white military operations against countries that harboured ANC military bases.

Such sanctions would have to be enforced by South Africa's trading partners both in Europe and in North America. Clearly such sanctions would have enormous political, social and economic costs. They would cause job losses inside South Africa and could subject the black population to considerable hardship.

The job losses and economic damage to the frontline states would be caused in several ways. First, there were many migrant workers in Mozambique, Lesotho, Malawi and Zimbabwe who were dependent on their employment in South Africa in order to support their families. Second, these workers were paid in foreign currency, of which their government got a percentage in taxes. In 1988 unemployment in Mozambique was running at over 40 per cent. In Zimbabwe it was at least 20 per cent, while a number of the other frontline states were either unable or unwilling to publish such data.

South Africa was also indirectly able to influence the transportation of the imports and exports of frontline states. This was because anti-Marxist guerrillas in Angola and

Mozambique frequently closed the main railway lines, which in turn also hit landlocked Zambia and Zimbabwe. Even when the lines were open, most of the frontline states needed to send goods through South African ports. On occasion, the Pretoria government could delay the delivery of goods, if they felt that Zimbabwe or Zambia was being too vocal in its criticism of South Africa.

Sanctions could also lead to loss of jobs in Western Europe, Japan and North America in the event of the interruption of the supplies of vital steel alloys. The job losses would be in the areas of engine-building for aircraft, the manufacture of computers and other items.

It was argued by the pro-sanctions lobby that such job losses and other suffering was a price worth paying in order to bring about the ending of apartheid. It was further argued that sanctions had contributed to the demise of white minority rule in Rhodesia and would have worked against Italy in the 1930s if sanctions had been extended to cover oil.

The pro-sanctions lobby pointed out that the ANC and the leaders of the frontline states openly called for sanctions against South Africa and said that they were prepared to pay the price of such suffering as they might incur. Opponents of sanctions pointed to the fact that the ANC had not had its mandate to speak for black South Africans tested in an election, and furthermore there were powerful sections of the black community opposed to the introduction of sanctions.

Those against sanctions argued that they were also opposed to the principle of inflicting such damage on the economies of South Africa, its neighbours and the possibility of job losses in North America and Western Europe. Opponents of sanctions argued that the most effective way of external actors in-fluencing progressive change in South Africa was to base their policies on constructive engagement. In any case, they argued, sanctions would not work because there were too many ways of circumventing them as third parties would be prepared to break such sanctions, either for financial gain or because of ideological sympathy. To support this contention, it was claimed that there had been a number of countries who had helped to break the mandatory United Nations arms embargo.

Those who opposed sanctions also wished for a pluralist government to follow the ending of apartheid. They wanted the ANC to have a role in such a government but not to be the sole party of government. Such people wished to see a prominent role for both the liberal white opposition and also for the Zulu-dominated Inkatha movement. Most of the socialist parties in Western Europe, black pressure groups, the Soviet Union and its allies and many prominent politicians in the Third World tended to support the ANC and so supported the imposition of sanctions against the South African government. Other supporters of sanctions included the Scandinavian countries and some of the former white British dominions such as Canada, Australia and New Zealand. Both Australia and New Zealand had socialist governments and Australia and Canada were major exporters of uranium and other minerals, which made them economic rivals of South Africa; their mining lobbies were vocal advocates of sanctions.

Most of the conservative parties in Western Europe and North America opposed sanctions. The British Conservative Party under Margaret Thatcher's leadership and the German Christian Democrats under Helmut Kohl, while being opposed to apartheid, were also opposed to sanctions. Although the American government under President Reagan opposed sanctions against South Africa, the domestic pressure from Congress (including both Republicans and Democrats) was so strong that the American government introduced a limited package of sanctions in the mid-1980s.

The governments of Britain and Germany had other reasons for opposing sanctions. Although estimates have varied, the implementation of mandatory comprehensive sanctions against South Africa could cost Britain some 70 000 jobs. Roughly 800 000 white South Africans hold British passports and have the right of entry to Britain. British governments cannot ignore the effect of such a large immigration of whites on race relations. The flight of the Algerian whites to the south of France in the early 1960s has provided a ready source of support for radical right-wing groups and racist terrorist groups. Clearly the influx of such a large group of South African whites to Britain might have similar implications.

One of the key areas where the effectiveness of sanctions was debated was the arms question. The South African arms industry had been self-sufficient in the production of small arms but was dependent on external sources for tanks, aircraft, naval vessels and advanced weapons systems. The South

African government set up ARMSCOR as a weapons procurement and development corporation. The South Africans were able to purchase weapons from the French and British until the compulsory United Nations arms embargo in 1977, but thereafter arms supplies continued to reach South Africa from sympathetic countries in the Far East, the Middle East and Latin America.

The arms embargo also stimulated the growth of a substantial domestic arms industry and the South Africans were able to attract scientists to work on their weapons programmes. The embargo did not prevent the South Africans from developing nuclear or chemical weapons nor did it stop them developing the G-5 and G-6 assault guns, which they were able to sell for export in the mid-1980s. This is not to say that the arms embargo caused no difficulties for successive South African governments. ARMSCOR had to resort to expensive subterfuges to circumvent the arms embargo in order to obtain spare parts for weapons. Because it was so difficult to obtain replacements for equipment that was damaged or destroyed, the South African military had to be very careful in its operations in order to minimize losses of equipment. This was particularly so in the case of aircraft and helicopters. By 1990 South Africa's arms exports were earning around $1 billion.

The prohibition of new loans to South Africa also caused substantial disruption to the South African economy. As the economy was dependent on capital imports for growth, the ban on new loans prevented such expansion at a time when demographic pressure needed it. Western dependence on a number of South African minerals has meant that these have often been exempted from sanctions in the past. This is particularly the case for minerals necessary for high-quality steel production, such as manganese, chromium, vanadium and silicon. There are other minerals that have such strategic importance that sanctions against them were never likely to have been enforced. These included asbestos, platinum, vermiculite, baddeleyite and nickel. Although Western Europe and North America could find alternative sources of gold, diamonds, uranium and copper when the market prices of such minerals were depressed, the constraints on uranium made the Western mining companies unwilling to pursue such exploration in the countries that had the largest reserves such as Canada and Australia. Seeking alternatives to some of the other minerals such as vanadium, platinum and baddeleyite were so expensive that they were not worth consideration.

Sanctions and Sport

In 1977 the Gleneagles Agreement was signed discouraging sporting contacts between Commonwealth countries and South Africa. Many sporting links with South Africa had already been suspended because of hostility to apartheid. For example, links with South African cricket were largely severed after the D'Oliveira affair in the 1960s. Basil D'Oliveira, a coloured South African who had settled in Britain, had played an important part in saving the Ashes during the 1967 season between England and Australia. D'Oliveira was subsequently picked for the England party that was to tour South Africa during the winter. The South African Prime Minister and former Nazi sympathizer B. J. Vorster condemned the inclusion of D'Oliveira in the party and the tour was cancelled.

If Western countries were not prepared to play sport in accordance with the Verwoerdian concept of apartheid, then the South African government under Vorster was quite prepared to do without international sporting links. There were no further England tours of South Africa, nor South African tours of England. Relations continued between South African and British rugby teams for longer but the effect of sporting isolation led towards the slow but gradual phasing out of apartheid in sport during the 1970s and 1980s. The South Africans last participated in the Olympic Games in 1960 but cricket and rugby were always the most important sports to the Afrikaners and athletics, boxing and soccer were of much less significance. Sports such as soccer were almost a preserve of black South Africans.

A number of black African countries threatened to boycott Olympic and Commonwealth Games meetings in the 1980s because several of the white states allowed sporting contacts with South Africa to continue. There was no doubt that, in the case of sport, sanctions and international pressures played an important part in helping to bring about the abolition of apartheid in sport in South Africa. The question of sporting links with South Africa was again raised in the 1980s with both the Zola Budd affair and the unofficial England cricket tour. Zola Budd was an exceptionally talented athlete who had

British relations and so was considered eligible for selection to the British national team. In the past, other South Africans had played for England, such as Basil D'Oliveira, Tony Greig and Allan Lamb, who had all played cricket for the English national side. Budd, however, was the victim of sustained harassment by anti-apartheid protesters and consequently she chose to spend much of her spare time back in South Africa. Continued pressure by anti-apartheid groups led her to return permanently to South Africa.

Further protests from the anti-apartheid movement greeted an unofficial England cricket tour led by Mike Gatting in 1990. This tour was organized by Dr Ali Bacher in order to show how much sport in South Africa was now free from apartheid. Bacher himself had long been a prominent opponent of apartheid and insisted that black groups in South Africa be allowed to protest at the grounds where Gatting's team was playing. However, the protests were such that the last two games were called off.

The Future of Sanctions

Throughout the 1980s there was growing opposition both in Western Europe and North America to the South African government's policies of apartheid. There were a number of reasons for this opposition. In the first place, there was substantial moral revulsion against the very concept of apartheid by the clergy and the intelligentsia. However, the most significant group behind the anti-apartheid movement was the black civil rights movement. Many of the black groups in the United States and Western Europe felt that their own governments were no longer sympathetic to their sectional needs. Some of these critics believed not only that the conservative policies of Margaret Thatcher and Ronald Reagan were sympathetic to the racist views of apartheid but that the only Achilles' heel of British and American conservatism was on the racial question. So opposition to Western policies towards South Africa was based on domestic political considerations as much as on an interest on foreign policy.

Yet for all the talk of sanctions, French imports from South Africa doubled between 1985 and 1990 (to over $600 million), while French exports to South Africa increased by over 20 per cent. The figures from Germany were even more startling.

German exports to South Africa increased by over 50 per cent ($3.5 million) while Germany increased her imports from South Africa by more than 30 per cent to over $1.6 billion.

In 1991 it seemed that the leadership of the ANC were prepared to contemplate ending their calls for sanctions, but at their conference in Johannesburg opposition from the rank and file strongly opposed such moves. Nevertheless, such opposition may well have reflected concern at the rising conflict between the ANC, Inkatha and AZAPO (successor to the Black Consciousness Movement) for dominance within the black community. There was concern among the ANC cadres that the violence in the townships was orchestrated by whites in order to weaken the positions of the black groups in future negotiations. It was felt that until this political violence had subsided the demand for sanctions should remain.

Clearly, as negotiations continue in the 1990s between the ANC, Inkatha and the South African government, demands for the removal of sanctions may increase; even if the ANC leadership wish to relax sanctions in order to relax tension between the power blocs, opposition from the rank and file of the ANC may prevent them from doing so. Until such time as the black population achieve what they perceive to be a fair share of political power, the issue of sanctions against the Pretoria government will remain on the agenda.

The Interests of White Labour

The white labour unions face a perennial problem, caught between two powerful groups: the white employers above them and the black workers below them. In order to secure their position as independent actors, they had to ensure that the system guaranteed them certain statutory rights over and above the black workers. Likewise, they were always mindful of occasions in the past, such as the mining strike on the Rand in the 1920s, when the employers and the government had used the armed forces against them.

The white workers remembered that they had shared the same living standards as the black workers in the recent past and that the Afrikaners in particular had endured horrific poverty during the 1930s. Consequently, the white working class had the largest interest in the establishment and maintenance of apartheid. This made the task of forging a common interest between white and black workers extremely difficult because the white workers perceived no common interest with the black workers. If black living standards rose, then they were likely to do so at the expense of white working class living standards. If black living standards fell, this was of no interest to the white working class unless their standards fell too. In most cases, the rise in the living standards of one group was at the expense of the other.

In the 1960s the rise in the living standards of the white workers was achieved by holding down the costs of black wages, while in the 1970s and 1980s the rises in black living standards were achieved as the living standards of the whites declined. In the 1980s it was the white unions that opposed the increase in the number of apprenticeships and the opening up of more areas of skilled employment to blacks. Yet the shortage of white skilled labour meant that, one way or another, more blacks were going to become skilled workers. Industry solved the problem by renaming the category of work and employing blacks to do the new jobs. However, they were usually paid less for doing it, while the whites were promoted to a supervisory grade that often meant more money but less work.

In 1979 over 15000 white workers organized a strike to protest against the advances made by black workers at the O'Kiep copper mines. This strike was a failure because the employers refused to compromise with the workers and neither the government nor the National Party was prepared to intervene on the side of the white workers. Organized by the White Mine Workers Union, the strike's failure led many senior figures in the union to doubt the National Party. A number of prominent figures in the union, such as Arrie Paulus, subsequently joined the Conservative Party.

The area that caused most concern for the white working class was the public sector, particularly the civil service. The Afrikaners, who had been poor in the pre-1939 period, had achieved a degree of affluence by the 1960s and most of them had done this through civil service employment. Jobs in the civil service were not only well paid but also carried very generous pensions, the provision of which placed a substantial burden on public expenditure. A leading South African academic, Dr A. D. Wassenaar, wrote a very critical book about pension provision in the public sector entitled *En Route to*

Fairyland. Wassenaar argued that the returns from the government pensions were far too good for the contributions paid into them. He further argued that the system was untenable as a long-term arrangement and would need to be radically altered.

As the Conservative Party grew in strength during the 1980s, it was from the white working class of manual and low-paid civil servants that its support emerged. Many white workers feared that if the blacks got control of the civil service, they would staff it with blacks only, thus denying the poor whites their source of income and affluence.

The Black Workers

Until 1979 successive South African governments had viewed black unionization with varying degrees of hostility. Under the 1948 Industrial Conciliation Act, the black population was effectively excluded from the negotiating sphere of the labour relations arena. One of the first decisions of the National government under Malan was to crush any vestige of black unionism and to ensure that the major trade unions were under white and more specifically Afrikaner control.

The Industrial Conciliation Act was part of a broader strategy of repression directed at African political groups. The Suppression of Communism Act (1950) attacked not only the South African Communist Party and the African National Congress but also the concept of multiracial trade unionism. The government claimed that action against the ANC was justified because of the Programme of Action adopted at the 1949 ANC conference. The Programme of Action called for mass protests against the discriminatory legislation introduced by the National Party after 1948 and indeed between 1950 and 1952 there was extensive popular protest by the blacks, Asians and coloureds against the apartheid legislation.

These protests were met with a stern response from the security forces, with over 8000 people being arrested and charged with a variety of offences. Police in the Eastern Cape area made the highest number of arrests. This was partly because it was the communists who had built up the black trade unions in the Port Elizabeth and Eastern Cape area. The area contained some of the worst poverty in South Africa and had a tradition of organization and unionization. Consequently, the trade unions were highly politicized and strike action was seen as both a political and economic form of protest. On account of their prominent role in trade union activity, both the Communist Party and the ANC received strong support: if the government could not destroy this support, it could at least crush the visible signs of such popular protest.

Changes in the criminal and administrative law meant that after 1952 it became almost impossible to continue industrial action in protest against the policies of the Malan government. Thereafter, most blacks were faced with migratory labour, and many of their union leaders were either arrested or served with banning orders. The subsequent Labour Relations Act of 1956 severely crippled the black unions for almost two decades because, although black trade unions were not made illegal, the changes in industrial relations legislation made it very difficult for them to operate. The procedure for calling strikes was made ever more difficult: strikes in essential services were declared illegal and multiracial unions were effectively prohibited. Yet, despite these legislative changes, the number of unofficial strikes grew during the late 1950s. A further wave of protests followed against the pass laws but the protests fell away after the state crackdown on all opposition following the shooting of over fifty demonstrators outside the police barracks at Sharpeville in March 1960. It was to be 1969 before black trade union militancy was to become a major force in South African politics.

In 1969 strikes in the Durban area led to a sustained wave of industrial unrest in the greater Durban area and subsequently also in the Eastern Cape. There were recurring strikes in both these areas in the early 1970s because of poor wages and conditions but also because of growing inflation in the economy. In 1973 the gold mines in the Witwatersrand area were hit by a wave of strikes and a number of miners were killed following clashes with the security forces. Many foreign miners from Malawi, Mozambique and Lesotho were repatriated as a result of taking strike action and many black South African miners were summarily dismissed.

As a result of the growing number of strikes, the government set up the Wiehahn Commission in 1977 to investigate the deterioration in industrial relations. The commission reported in 1979 and embarked on a programme of radical reforms. It recommended that black unions should become registered and entitled to participate in industrial disputes to the same degree as white unions. This was enacted in the Industrial Conciliation Amendment Act (1979). Other recommendations of the Wiehahn Commission were that the restrictions on multiracial unions should be rescinded and that statutory job reservation for whites should be ended. This implicitly meant that more blacks should be given apprenticeships for skilled work although this was required in any case because of the shortage of skilled labour among the white community.

The trade unions in South Africa are grouped together in a series of federations that also signify political allegiance. The South African Confederation of Labour (SACOL) represents the majority of white workers but has lost much of its political influence as the National Party has shifted its power base of support away from working-class Afrikaners. The Trade Union Congress of South Africa (TUCSA) is a multiracial union grouping that symbolized moderate opposition to the National Party between the 1950s and the 1980s. Its membership is estimated to have exceeded 400 000 by the middle of the 1980s.

The Federation of South African Trade Unions (FOSATU) was set up in 1979 as a multiracial body, although the majority of its members are black. It saw enormous expansion in the early 1980s and it benefited considerably from the Wiehahn reforms. Its membership grew from under 30 000 in 1979 to over 150 000 by the mid-1980s. The Council of South African Unions (CUSA), a black trade union federation opposed to the National Party, claimed a membership of over 250 000 members by the mid-1980s.

The Azanian Confederation of Trade Unions (AZACTU) claimed a membership of 75 000 members and was politically aligned towards the Black Consciousness Movement. The most significant development in the 1980s was the formation of the Congress of South African Trade Unions (COSATU) in 1985. COSATU, which claimed a membership of over 500 000, became significant because of its links with the ANC and the United Democratic Front (UDF). Jay Naidoo became the first general secretary of COSATU and Elijah Barayi its first president. COSATU brought together not only the FOSATU grouping but a number of unions disaffiliated from other federations to join COSATU. One of the most prominent unions in the COSATU federation was the National Union of Mineworkers, led by Cyril Ramaphosa. Ramaphosa had built up his reputation following a series of truculent battles with the Chamber of Mines and in particular with the Anglo-American group.

In 1986 COSATU issued a joint manifesto with the ANC in Lusaka, while linking up with the UDF inside South Africa. The Zulu-based Inkatha movement became concerned at this link-up between its chief political rivals and the most powerful trade union that claimed a sizeable Zulu following. In response to this perceived challenge, Inkatha launched its own trade union, the United Workers Union of South Africa (UWUSA), in May 1986.

Although the number of strikes by black unions rose during the first half of the 1980s, these declined in the second half as the South African economy faced mounting problems. The black trade unions found a space to grow in the political arena while the ANC remained a proscribed organization, but with the unbanning of the ANC the black unions may find their future role diminished.

Chapter 5

THE INTERNAL OPPOSITION

The black community in South Africa has always opposed the policies of apartheid. The opposition to white minority rule has been divided by beliefs on strategy, beliefs on the relationship between blacks and other races and ethnic groups in the liberation movement. Opposition has also taken many different forms, such as the non-violent opposition advocated by sections of the clergy, in particular Archbishop Desmond Tutu. In the 1980s the Congress of South African Trade Unions (COSATU) became prominent in opposing apartheid policies in the area of industrial relations and housing. The United Democratic Front (UDF) began to galvanize the urban black population in the townships, until the government prohibited the organization from participating in political activities. The most dramatic change in the state of the South African opposition came on 2 February 1989, when President de Klerk lifted the ban on the South African Communist Party, the African National Congress and the Pan-Africanist Congress. This opened the way for those organizations to participate openly in politics for the first time in thirty years.

African opposition to the European presence in South Africa had continued from the earliest days of settlement in the Cape. Major battles were fought towards the end of the nineteenth century in order to subdue the Zulu nation. However, the greater resources of the Europeans in terms of arms and ammunition ensured their ultimate victory. Nevertheless the settler conquest was never considered to be final and irrevocable. The most successful opposition to the segregationist policies was achieved by the Indian Congress, led by Mohandas K. Gandhi. Gandhi adopted the tactics of *satyagraha* (non-violent resistance) against the government of General Smuts.

The landmark in black African politics was the founding of the African National Congress in 1912. The Act of Union, signed in Bloemfontein in 1910, absolved Britain of its responsibilities for the domestic affairs of the Union of South Africa. A number of leading blacks, concerned at the lack of black rights under the Act of Union, called a conference that ended with the formation of the ANC. Many of the founders of the ANC were clergy, members of the legal profession and teachers. Its first president was Dr John Dube who advocated that the Africans should try to persuade the liberal white politicians of the day to remove the laws discriminating against them. However, this was not to be the case and in 1913 the Native Land Act further restricted the right of blacks to own or lease land.

The ANC actively supported the British war effort in 1914, despite its disillusionment with the British government's indifference to the plight of South African blacks. Africans volunteered for service but were not accepted for combat roles. This experience was a considerable humiliation not only for the black soldiers but also for the leaders of the ANC. The post-war unemployment led to a growing fear among members of the white working class that blacks would be a major source of competition for jobs. This in turn meant that the tactics of the ANC were even less likely to be successful in persuading the white government to ameliorate black conditions. The ANC thus had a declining influence on both the white and the black communities, the major beneficiary of which was the Industrial and Commercial Workers Union led by Clemens Kadalie.

Although the South African Communist Party initially helped Kadalie, he soon rejected its support as he moved to the right, while the Communist Party turned its attention to the ANC. However, its flirtation with communism cost the ANC the support of its rural conservative wing. In 1930 Dr Pixley Seme was elected as the new head of the ANC but, like Dube, he was a moderate and circumstances were against him. Neither Dube nor Seme wished to engage in the politics of popular protest, thus leaving the ANC with no policies for pursuing its objectives other than that of trying to petition other whites of the justice of their cause. In 1940 Dr Albert Xuma became president of the ANC and was to remain so until 1949 when he was replaced by Dr James Moroka.

Xuma's leadership of the ANC faced a number of challenges during the 1940s from younger members of the organization who believed that his tactics were politically ineffective in improving the condition of the blacks. Throughout the 1940s there was a series of strikes, boycotts and other local protests by blacks in opposition to the discriminatory measures that they faced. The most significant of these demonstrations were the bus boycotts in Alexandria and the squatters movement in Johannesburg. The bus boycotts were caused by the fact that, under housing laws, blacks could not live in the 'white' cities and hence they required bus transportation to get from their homes to their places of work in the city. However, they were not allowed to organize their own transportation or bus companies and this gave the white bus operators a monopoly position. The blacks reckoned that fare increases were more than they could afford and consequently they opted for a boycott of the buses.

The protest of the squatters was caused by the acute shortage of housing for blacks in the Johannesburg area. This shortage led many blacks to squat on unoccupied land surrounding existing black townships. Unfortunately for them, the area was designated as white and the authorities eventually broke up their settlement.

Opposition to the conservative leadership of the ANC came principally from its youth league (usually known as the Congress Youth League (CYL)). The driving force of the CYL was initially Anton Lembede, but, after his death in 1947, Nelson Mandela and Oliver Tambo became more prominent. Lembede argued cogently for more popular protest and demonstrations to be organized against the white governments, and in this he was supported by Mandela and Tambo. Both Mandela and Tambo, along with Walter Sisulu, were elected to the national executive of the ANC in the 1950s and they were to devise a more active political strategy for the ANC.

Lembede had been primarily in favour of the Africans developing black organizations and of a strategy that involved more mass demonstrations and protests. He was very suspicious of whites and in particular of the white members of the Communist Party.

Throughout the 1950s the debate inside the ANC revolved around three issues. First, there was the question of how the organization should proceed in terms of strategy. Was it viable for it to pursue policies of non-violence in the face of the repression meted out by the security forces at its peaceful demonstrations? Second, there was the question of the links between the African National Congress and the South African Communist Party. Many of the younger members of the ANC, such as Nelson Mandela and Oliver Tambo, were concerned that their older leaders were falling under the excessive influence of the Communist Party. They were perturbed about this relationship because they feared that the interests of the liberation of the blacks and the long-term problem of the relationship between the races in South Africa would take second place to the communist struggle for power and the needs of Soviet foreign policy.

The third major issue that divided the ANC leadership overlapped with that of relations with the Communist Party and was the question of the role of whites in the anti-apartheid conflict. Some remembered the white communists during the 1922 mining strike on the Rand, who made their appeals to the white working class in terms of white racial solidarity against the blacks. Others, such as Robert Sobukwe, argued that a preoccupation with white fears and trying to influence the more enlightened whites was the chief reason for the failure of the ANC to improve the lot of Africans while Dube and Seme had led the organization. Sobukwe argued that blacks needed to define their needs and policies in their own terms and for the benefit of the African population. This perspective drew its inspiration from the ideas of Anton Lembede and such ideas were to become popular again with the rise of the Black Consciousness Movement in the 1970s. However, as his disillusionment with the ANC grew, Sobukwe left the organization in order to form the Pan-Africanist Congress in 1959.

Mandela viewed Sobukwe's ideas as unhelpful in the search for a common identity for all South Africans. Whereas most of the white populations in Africa had only been on the continent for a short time, the South African whites had lived on the continent for over 400 years and had nowhere else to go. Furthermore, the whites still held enormous military power and economic resources on their side.

From Defiance to Rivonia

In 1949 the ANC adopted its Programme For Action at its annual conference at Bloemfontein in the Orange Free State. This programme was essentially a declaration of intent that the new leadership of the ANC, Mandela, Tambo and Sisulu, were not going to be content with petitioning the white parliament for the redress of grievances. The ANC, like the rest of the black, coloured and Asian population, was horrified by the apartheid legislation of the Malan government after 1948, but it was not until 1950 that it was able to plan and organize large-scale protests in opposition to the National government.

Just as Gandhi had organized non-violent protests against discriminatory legislation in 1908, so the ANC believed that it should use a similar strategy of passive resistance. The ANC launched the Defiance Campaign, which lasted from 1950 to 1952, and it focused its aim on mobilizing the black population against the new restrictions of the Malan government. They were able to do this because the blacks had many legitimate grievances and it was clear to the majority of blacks that the National Party was not interested in trying to rectify these problems.

The Defiance Campaign established the ANC as the main political party of the African population and it showed what Africans could do when they were organized. At a stroke it discredited the old policies of Dube, Seme and Xuma, who had reckoned that Africans lacked the discipline to stage such peaceful demonstrations. The ANC leadership hoped that non-violent protest and permitting themselves to be arrested (as Gandhi had done in India and as Dr Martin Luther King was to do in the United States in the 1950s and 1960s) would clog up both the courts and the jails. This did not happen because the government and the security forces used their draconian public order legislation to attack the ANC and disrupt their protest movement.

In 1952 Chief Albert Luthuli, a Zulu and a lay preacher, was elected as the new president of the ANC. As a Christian, Luthuli was committed to a strategy of peaceful change but he was nevertheless determined to pursue a more activist campaign for change than Dube, Seme or Xuma. Luthuli was also hopeful that many whites could be persuaded of the immorality of the apartheid system and of the desirability of its abolition.

In the aftermath of the defiance campaign, a number of the ANC leadership thought that the struggle against apartheid needed a political movement that covered all races. Luthuli was encouraged that the whites did not have a homogeneous position on race relations and that at least a few were sympathetic to the ANC's cause. This led to the founding of the South African Congress of Democrats in 1953. This group was dominated by left-wing members of the white community and it included many trade unionists. The Congress of Democrats was to become more prominent in the ensuing years, a development that was to cause concern to both white liberals and many blacks. The white liberals were opposed to the growing pro-Soviet stance of the Congress of Democrats at a time when the Soviet Union was carrying out its own campaign of repression in Eastern Europe, particularly in East Germany and Hungary. For many blacks, the position of any whites in the anti-apartheid struggle was problematic. Some blacks, who were subsequently to form the Pan-Africanist Congress, wondered if they might not be swapping one set of white masters for another.

In 1955 a gathering of a number of opposition groups met at Kliptown, near Johannesburg, and agreed the Freedom Charter. The charter seemed to be a basic declaration of human rights but both white liberals and black radicals remained suspicious of the pre-eminent role of the Congress of Democrats. The Kliptown conference ended with a raid by the security forces, which aimed to gather as much material and documents on the leaders of the various opposition groups as possible.

The excuse used by the security forces to justify the raid was that the gathering might have constituted treasonable activity because of its call for drastic change in the nature of the South African state. In 1956, 156 anti-apartheid campaigners were arrested and charged with treason. These included Luthuli, Mandela and other leading members of the ANC. This trial continued for four years, although in 1957 the charges against sixty-one of the defendants were dropped and in 1958 the charges against a further sixty campaigners were dropped. When the case finally came to trial, the remaining defendants were found not guilty in early 1961. Many anti-apartheid campaigners believed that the treason trial was simply an act of harassment against the ANC and its allies.

The treason trial led many among the ANC leadership to question the continuation of non-violent protest alone. One of the factors that did most to change black perceptions about the use of violence was the Sharpeville incident in 1960. Although the ANC was a disciplined organization, the same was not the case for their rivals, the PAC. The PAC was more interested in the principle of mass mobilization and in 1960, along with the ANC, organized a series of demonstrations against the pass laws, which governed the movement of blacks. One of these demonstrations was at Sharpeville near Johannesburg. A very large number of protestors surrounded the local police station in order to give themselves up and be arrested as part of the campaign of non-violent resistance. Although the protest was intended to be peaceful, it was to end in tragedy with over fifty of the demonstrators being killed by police gunfire. A number of police had panicked and, fearing that they were going to be killed by the large African crowd, opened fire on the demonstrators.

Verwoerd's government acted to crush the anti-pass law demonstrations and arrested many of the ANC and PAC leaders. With the draconian public order legislation that it had at its disposal, it was easy for the South African government to charge and convict the leaders of the African opposition. A state of emergency was declared and the ANC, the PAC and the South African Communist Party were all proscribed.

Nelson Mandela and a number of other ANC leaders came to the conclusion that there was little future for any strategy of non-violent resistance to apartheid and they decided to go underground and establish the nucleus of a guerrilla force. This military organization was named Umkhonto We Sizwe (Spear of the Nation) and its title was usually abbreviated to MK. The PAC also established its own military wing, Poqo. MK's military strategy was aimed at hitting government buildings, especially those associated with the administration of the apartheid laws. The ANC was concerned to avoid the loss of civilian life and was also keen to avoid armed struggle becoming an incitement for blacks to kill whites. This was not the case with the PAC's military cadre, Poqo, which liked the idea of racial polarization, believing that it would foster the growth of racial consciousness and self-confidence in the black community.

For all the enthusiasm of the black opposition, the South African government had well-trained security forces and initial successes for the guerrillas were short-lived. Mandela was arrested in 1962 and most of the rest of the MK leadership was subsequently captured at a farm in Rivonia in 1963. The South African police had developed a large number of informants in most of the opposition groups and consequently managed to arrest most of the internal leaders of the black opposition. In 1964 Nelson Mandela, Walter Sisulu and Govan

Mbeki were all found guilty of sabotage and sentenced to life imprisonment. Mandela was to serve most of his sentence on Robben Island prison and was not brought back to the South African mainland until 1982.

Sobukwe and the PAC

The PAC was founded in 1959 and Robert Sobukwe was elected its first president. The formation of the PAC reflected a growing concern among some members of the ANC about both the organization's philosophy and political strategy. The membership of the PAC had a number of views on their definition of African. For some, Africa was for black Africans and the whites should return to Europe. For others, African meant all those who lived there on the continent of Africa and that included those who were white.

However, the PAC was agreed on two points: first, that it was the blacks who would determine the identity of the anti-apartheid movement and second, the most important part of their political strategy was to be the mobilization of the black masses. The PAC also believed that considerations of white sensitivities about such a strategy were not to be taken as an excuse for refraining from acts of either non-violent or violent resistance should the struggle require the adoption of such tactics.

By 1960 the membership of the PAC had grown to just over 30 000 members, often drawing its support from areas where the ANC was weak, divided or where its leadership on the ground was unpopular. One area where a number of these factors existed was the Western Cape. The PAC leadership, such as Sobukwe and Potlake Leballo, were extremely suspicious of the role of whites in the anti-apartheid struggle. They distrusted the communists, whom they believed were only out to further their own aims and objectives, while they reckoned that too many of the liberals were unwilling to endorse tactics of mass demonstrations. In general, the PAC believed that the influence of whites in the anti-apartheid campaign confused and hindered the struggle; among the people it attacked as having a detrimental effect on its cause were Bishop Trevor Huddleston and Patrick Duncan, the son of a former governor-general of South Africa. In both cases it was obliged to reverse its earlier judgments.

In 1960 the PAC and ANC found the pass laws at the top of their list of grievances. The PAC was keen to mobilize protests against these laws by mass demonstrations and by having its members arrested in order to congest the courts. On several occasions, they surrounded police stations and offered themselves for arrest in the time-honoured manner of the tradition of non-violent resistance. The PAC leadership were warned by the security forces that such a tactic was dangerous because it might be considered as an attack on a police station. The warnings were ambiguous because on the one hand they were interpreted as a threat of what might happen should the police wish to take a hostile interpretation of events; on the other hand, it was also a warning of the danger of what might occur in the event of a genuine misunderstanding. In the case of the Sharpeville incident, it would seem that a mixture of fear and inexperience on the part of the policemen concerned led to the tragic shootings in which so many peaceful demonstrators were killed.

In the aftermath of the Sharpeville incident, the South African government acted to crush further opposition from both the ANC and the PAC. The Sharpeville incident and the subsequent proscription of the PAC led many in the organization to question the future of a strategy of non-violent resistance. Like the ANC, the PAC also formed its own military wing, Poqo. Having abandoned the strategy of non-violent resistance, Poqo embraced the armed struggle with enthusiasm. Unlike the ANC, which initially took care in its selection of targets, the PAC launched its military attacks against whites in general, anyone vaguely suspected of being an informer and even members of rival opposition groups.

Poqo was responsible for much of the anti-government violence between 1960 and 1962. Thereafter, the police managed to arrest many key activists from both the military and the political wings of the movement. Sobukwe's arrest and imprisonment was a severe blow to the PAC as it deprived the movement of its most influential strategist. From the mid-1960s both the PAC and Poqo were reduced to making plans in exile as their ability to act within South Africa was dramatically curtailed.

The PAC suffered from a number of problems that were to prevent it from becoming a major player in South African politics. The organization lacked the support of a major backer, a factor that was of crucial importance to any group that faced exile from its own country. While the ANC received support from the Soviet Union and most of its client states, the PAC only received periodic support from communist China because the latter made the point of supporting any rival anti-Russian national liberation movement. The PAC had little ideological common ground with communist China, therefore the Chinese always viewed the PAC with caution.

The PAC faced further difficulties because it did not enjoy good relationships with other African liberation movements, including those supported by the Chinese, such as Frelimo in Mozambique and ZANU (PF) in Rhodesia. The reason for this series of bad relationships was caused by two factors: corruption and ill-discipline within the PAC itself, and the fact that the PAC allied with rival liberation groups in both Angola and Mozambique. In Angola, the PAC allied with the ill-fated FNLA, while in Mozambique they allied with the Comite Revolucionario de Moçambique (COREMO) an anti-Frelimo organization. In the Angolan civil war the FNLA were swiftly crushed by the Cuban military, which intervened to install the MPLA, while in Mozambique COREMO were never a serious challenge to Frelimo. As a result of its poor relations with the governing parties in both Angola and Mozambique, it was very difficult for the PAC to infiltrate guerrillas into South Africa from its bases in Tanzania. In any case, the PAC guerrillas received little military training and the organization lacked the funds to purchase adequate supplies of arms and ammunition. Poqo faced more serious obstacles to military action because of its lack of organization inside South Africa.

All these factors meant that PAC exiles spent most of their time plotting and feuding amongst themselves. In Sobukwe's absence, the PAC leader was Potlake Leballo and most of the faction fighting in the 1960s and 1970s was between pro- and anti-Leballo supporters. His opponents accused him of auto-cratic leadership and corruption while they plotted against him, and this plotting included a number of assassination attempts. Leballo was succeeded by David Sibeko but the latter was assassinated in Tanzania in 1979 as part of an internal feud.

After Sibeko's death, Vus Make took over the leadership until he was replaced a year later by John Pokela. The death of Sobukwe in 1978 had been a blow to the PAC because it had removed their most able leader and the one to whom many members of the organization had looked for inspiration during the long years of exile.

In 1968 Poqo was renamed the Azanian People's Liberation Army but the change of name was to do little to improve its military capability. Throughout the 1980s the PAC continued to be haunted by allegations of corruption, inefficiency and internal feuding. In 1985 Johnson Mlambo was elected PAC president to replace Pokela but he was unable to solve the intractable problems that had so long damaged the organization. The PAC was unable to benefit from either the Soweto uprising in 1976 or from the mass protests following the unrest in the townships in the mid-1980s. In the 1990s the PAC was to remain in the background, unable to throw up any new leaders and unable to escape its black exclusivist ideology. Its military cadres were ineffective while its political wing lacked organization and was tainted with corruption.

The ANC: From Morogoro to Kabwe

The ANC was declared an illegal organization by the National government in 1960. This was a blow to the organization as it meant that the ANC was obliged to go underground and could no longer operate openly without exposing its members to arrest and imprisonment. The ANC had suspected that it might become proscribed and had taken the precaution of sending a number of its members abroad in order to ensure that it would have the nucleus of an organization at liberty in the event of the arrest of their leadership inside South Africa.

The ANC's long period of pursuing non-violent resistance came to an end because its leaders believed that such a strategy was no longer viable. The South African government had made it clear that it was not prepared to tolerate any form of protest to its policies of apartheid. Oliver Tambo was the head of the ANC's external mission whose function was to raise funds and to help organize international protests against the South African regime with other opposition groups. The ANC approached a number of sources for financial and logistical assistance; however, its representations to the Soviet Union and its allies proved to be more fruitful than those to the Western powers. Facilities for military training were offered by a number of African states but few of these countries possessed armed forces of an adequate calibre to match the training given to the South African armed forces.

The ANC set up a number of offices in Zambia, Tanzania and Britain with the major training bases being in Zambia and Tanzania. The ANC's military wing, Umkhonto We Sizwe (MK), initially intended to infiltrate guerrillas into South Africa via Botswana and Zambia but this became too difficult because the South African security forces were able to anticipate the main transit routes. Despite the fact that the main body of the MK leadership was arrested at Rivonia, guerrilla infiltration continued for a number of years, although with little effect in disrupting white political and military hegemony.

By 1968 it was clear that the military campaign of MK was not achieving its anticipated results. There were a number of reasons for this lack of success. In the first place the infiltration route to South Africa was long and hazardous without the sort of favourable geographic circumstances that were present on the Ho Chi Minh trail that linked northern and southern Vietnam. Second, the South African security forces had the opposition groups well permeated with informers, who provided invaluable intelligence on ANC and MK operations. Third, MK lacked good training and supplies for its members, and, finally, the ANC lacked a coherent strategy for toppling the National Party from power.

In 1969 an attempt was made to review these problems at the ANC's third consultative conference at Morogoro in Tanzania. The leadership of both the ANC and MK decided that their external mission would need serious reorganization not only in terms of political and military strategy but also in terms of organizational structure and membership. There was an intense debate about whether or not those of other races should be allowed to join the ANC and in particular about the role of whites within the organization. It concluded that an increased role for whites, coloureds and Asians within the national liberation movement would be beneficial, although restrictions on the role that whites could play would remain for some time.

The Morogoro conference also raised the perennial problem of bad morale among MK rank and file in the training camps and of the accusations of corruption aimed at a number of the leaders of the ANC mission in exile. There was little that could be done about the question of MK morale while infiltration into South Africa remained such a major problem. The issue of corruption among exiled ANC and MK leaders was one that was to return at periodic intervals to embarrass the leaderships of both organizations.

The ANC entered the 1970s with more optimism about the future. It was clear that the Portuguese were unable to maintain their African colonies indefinitely. Their armies were divided into too many theatres of operations, their conscripts were unhappy about service conditions and the cost of the wars was consuming a growing proportion of Portugal's public expenditure. Following the Portuguese military coup in 1974, the Portuguese army effectively gave up its counter-insurgency operations.

This was to be a major boon for the ANC and other liberation movements. Frelimo was to take power in Mozambique in 1974, while the Soviet- and Cuban-backed MPLA was to become the government of Angola in 1976. The accession to power of Frelimo in Mozambique meant that MK guerrillas were able to cross directly into South Africa via the Kruger National Park. The Frelimo victory greatly facilitated the war waged by Zimbabwean guerrillas and hastened the end of white rule in Rhodesia, thus significantly extending the borders for the South African security forces. Members of MK fought with both the MPLA and the Zimbabwean guerrillas and both countries provided financial, diplomatic and logistical support for the ANC's cause.

The ANC attained a certain amount of popular support among the black masses because it was the major opposition group fighting the South African government. Unlike the PAC, the ANC also made fortuitous alliances with the winning sides in the Mozambican and Angolan conflicts, although their relations with the ZANU (PF) group in Zimbabwe remained cool until the late 1980s. During the 1970s, despite the fact that the ANC leadership was either in exile or in prison, the ANC remained the organization to which many of the Black Consciousness supporters looked for inspiration, and following the Soweto uprising in 1976 it was to the ANC that most of the young exiles flocked as the organization with the largest presence in the frontline states.

In the early 1980s the Pretoria government began its policy of total strategy aimed at keeping the ANC and MK as far away from South African borders as possible. The Botha government also attempted to weaken any of the frontline states that were sympathetic to the ANC by supporting any anti-government guerrilla forces in those countries. The Nkomati Accord in 1984 between South Africa and Mozambique caused a reduction in the ANC presence in that country, but a year later MK guerrillas were once again infiltrating into South Africa via the Kruger National Park on the South Africa-Mozambique border. However, recruitment to the ANC was stimulated in 1984 following Botha's new constitution. In the next three years many young men and women would go into exile via Botswana or Lesotho in order to join the ANC.

In 1985 the ANC held their third consultative conference at Kabwe in Zambia. (As they were a banned organization, they were unable to hold an open conference in South Africa as they would have wished.) The ANC felt psychologically strengthened with the fall of each white minority regime, and with the fall of white Rhodesia in 1980 only South Africa and its Namibian satellite remained.

The Kabwe conference marked a significant turning-point in ANC strategy. Delegates from both the ANC and MK decided to move away from their traditional tactics of hitting military targets only and of mounting periodic attacks from their bases outside the country. After Kabwe, MK units were organized on a more regular basis inside South Africa in both the townships and the homelands. Although it was always difficult for the ANC to operate in KwaZulu because so many of the ANC cadres were Xhosa, the ANC was able to command sizeable support in both the Transkei and Ciskei. The conference also resolved to make the townships ungovernable and to destroy the ability of government-sponsored institutions to function there. This meant that both the MK and township radicals launched on a prolonged campaign of the assassination of local councillors, policemen, police informers and other political rivals. Many of those assassinated were killed by necklacing, that is by placing a petrol-soaked tyre round the neck of the victim and then igniting it. The Kabwe conference also emphasized the alliance between the United Democratic Front (UDF) and the ANC. This alliance meant that there were then three major power blocs in the black population, the largest being the ANC/UDF, the second Inkatha and the third the PAC and the Black Consciousness Movement.

During the 1980s the relationship between the ANC and MK began to change. MK became more powerful and its leadership more youthful and dynamic. Joe Slovo, the veteran communist, gave way to younger cadres such as Joe Modise and Chris Hani. Critics of the ANC still pointed to the large number of communists and members of the Xhosa tribe who held high office in the organization. On account of post-colonial Africa's troubled history of ethnic and tribal strife, other groups in South Africa remained concerned about the predominance of white communists and Xhosas within the ANC and MK.

Steve Biko and Black Consciousness

The black opposition in South Africa faced a number of dilemmas during the 1960s. The two major groups, the ANC and the PAC, were unable to mount an effective policy that was capable of challenging the National Party's control of the country. Their leaders were either in prison or in exile and their campaigns of armed struggle were ineffective. Some blacks decided to bide their time until one of the opposition movements was strong enough to take on the powers of the South African state. Others decided to join the administrations of the black homelands and work within the system, while others still were prepared to collaborate with the apartheid regime against the black opposition.

In the late 1960s a new generation of black groups emerged with Steve Biko and Barney Pityana as their most prominent spokesmen. These groups became known collectively as the Black Consciousness Movement (BCM). Biko rose to national attention when he led a break away from the National Union of South African Students, the multiracial student union organization. Biko's new group was the South African Students Organization (SASO). The second group associated with the Black Consciousness Movement was the Black People's Convention (BPC).

The Black Consciousness Movement had many ideas that were similar to those of the PAC. For example, they were opposed to the white liberals having a leading role in the anti-apartheid struggle. They argued that developing black pride and self-awareness had to be the first prerequisite in the struggle for black liberation. The BPC was not in favour of the armed struggle as an immediate priority but it believed that in the future it might become the only feasible strategy for attaining political and economic liberation. The BPC was formed in 1972 and although it was not proscribed by the government many of its leaders were banned under South African security legislation.

Biko and his followers busied themselves in a series of community programmes to build up community self-reliance. In 1976 Biko and a number of his followers were arrested and charged with subversion. Their trial was an attempt by the government to harass and silence another group of political opponents, and although Biko was not jailed a number of his colleagues were sentenced to terms of imprisonment. However, in August 1977, Biko was arrested by the security police and died several days later in police custody. Biko's death provoked an international outcry and contributed to the international isolation of South Africa.

With Biko dead, the Black Consciousness Movement became divided on future policies. Some BPC leaders argued that the blacks should model their strategies and tactics on those of the American civil rights movement under Dr Martin Luther King by continuing to use non-violent protests and tactics such as buyers' boycotts against shops that practised apartheid. Other BPC leaders argued that blacks needed to concentrate on building up their economic power within the capitalist system in order to make themselves independent of whites. Similar views to these were expressed in the United States in the 1920s by Marcus Garvey. Other BPC leaders simply acted as outlets for anti-white feelings and called for a war against the whites. They also defined black as referring only to Africans and not to coloureds and Asians. These views tended to draw on some of the militant views of Malcolm X, the black American radical of the 1960s. Some members of the BPC even argued that because racism and apartheid were so much a part of the capitalist system no liberation for the blacks would be possible until the entire system had been overthrown.

Therefore some of the Black Consciousness Movement joined the ANC, some the PAC, and others went into business. However there was one area where the Black Consciousness Movement had an important influence and that was in the Soweto protest in 1976. The BPC had fostered the idea of

119

black community politics and had given a number of community groups a much greater degree of organization and
confidence than they had previously possessed.

Black Consciousness had always had more support among
black intellectuals, student and youth groups rather than
among professionals, workers or peasants. Although the
Soweto revolt had a number of long-term structural causes, it
was the short-term trigger of the government's decision to
order that African students should be taught in Afrikaans that
sparked the student revolt in 1976. Such a decision on the part
of the government was extremely foolish because it was a
measure that the blacks regarded as provocative. It brought up
all the old issues of 'Bantu education' and the blacks were
determined that they were not going to be taught in the
language of the hated Afrikaners.

For some of the township youth, no education was preferable
to the fourth-rate education they received under the apartheid
system. The riots that rocked the townships left many
protesters dead and wounded while many more went into exile
to join one of the liberation movements. The protests also
helped to undermine government control of the townships
because although the security forces were able to contain the
unrest to the townships, they were unable to prevent the
unrest within these areas.

Yet Biko's death did not kill the Black Consciousness Movement. In 1978 the Azanian People's Organization was formed
and it adopted a radical anti-capitalist programme; in 1983 the
National Forum was established as a coalition of a number of
community-based but Black Consciousness-orientated groups.
One of the long-term effects of Black Consciousness' influence
was to be found in the fact that throughout the 1980s and
1990s, black groups became much better organized. This was
to be of enormous help to both the trade union movement and
the United Democratic Front in their struggles against the
National government after 1984.

Buthelezi and Inkatha

The ANC was by no means the only powerful black group to
oppose apartheid. The largest of the black ethnic groups were
the Zulus, who numbered over five million people. The Zulus
were a proud nation that had been the last to be defeated by

the European settlers in the late nineteenth century. Zulus played their part in the early ANC but in the early 1960s came to be suspicious of the dominant role played in the ANC by their arch-rivals the Xhosas. Even more worrying for the Zulus was concern that the ANC in particular and the anti-apartheid movement in general was being hijacked by the South African Communist Party.

Chief Buthelezi decided to form a distinctly Zulu organization in order both to oppose the apartheid system but also to prevent ANC and communist domination of the black opposition. Inkatha was formed in 1975 and was based in the Zulu homeland of KwaZulu and the urban townships of Natal. Inkatha opposes the ANC on a number of issues. It is pro-Western and virulently anti-communist. Inkatha opposes sanctions against South Africa as being detrimental to the cause of ending apartheid. Buthelezi did not think that the ANC mission in exile had the right to call for sanctions that would inflict substantial hardship on South African blacks when those in exile were not likely to be the ones doing the suffering.

The ANC did not suffer from significant ethnic dissension until 1960. Chief Albert Luthuli was a Zulu and Buthelezi himself had been a member of the ANC in his youth. However, the years of exile and the seemingly ineffective policies of the ANC led a number of blacks such as Buthelezi to consider using the homelands structure as a means of mobilizing political support against the apartheid system. Whereas some of the homelands leaders were manifestly puppets of the Pretoria government, Buthelezi was always his own man and indeed he called for the release of Nelson Mandela on many occasions.

The ANC for its part had initially supported Buthelezi as a popular internal black leader who was a trenchant critic of successive Nationalist governments. During the 1970s there was a division of opinion within the ANC over relations with Buthelezi and Inkatha. The external mission supported Buthelezi because KwaZulu and other Zulu-dominated areas were alongside most of South Africa's north-eastern borders. If Inkatha were to oppose the ANC then it had the power to bloc MK infiltration routes. Buthelezi had a series of private meetings with Oliver Tambo, the ANC president, but these were inconclusive. The core of the problem of Inkatha-ANC rivalry was the conflict between the rank and file supporters of both organizations and their desire for control of Natal. The ANC was not prepared to allow Inkatha a free hand in the area, while Inkatha was not prepared to allow the ANC to claim to be the sole legitimate representatives of black South Africa.

One of the factors that caused whites to fear black majority rule was the track record of black majority governments elsewhere in Africa, particularly those that had espoused the radical socialist and communist rhetoric that had characterized so many of the ANC policies of the 1970s. The massacres of whites that had occurred in Zaire, the economic collapse that had attended the Marxist regimes in Ethiopia, Angola and Mozambique all contributed to white fears about the possibility of a future black government in South Africa. This fear had made many whites not only refuse to contemplate the possibility of blacks in government but also to consider any serious options for sharing political power with South Africa's black majority.

Buthelezi had managed to break down this fear in a way that no other black leader had done. In the late 1970s he had convened an indaba with leaders of the white opposition and business community to consider alternative political structures to those of apartheid on the one hand, and on the other the one-party states which were so prevalent in the rest of sub-Saharan Africa.

The indaba produced a substantial report which advocated a form of consociational democracy (in general terms this implied that all the major political parties would have representatives taking part in government). Under Buthelezi's plan, the concept of power-sharing would be tried out in KwaZulu-Natal and if it was seen to be working, similar models could be tried in the rest of the country. The National Party leadership attacked this idea, partly because they were not prepared to share real power with the black community, but also in the hope that refusal to deal with Buthelezi might undercut his support and so weaken him for the future. Nevertheless, the Natal indaba won Buthelezi friends both in South Africa and abroad for his attempt to break the constitutional stalemate.

In the early 1980s Inkatha faced rivalry from the newly emergent United Democratic Front (UDF). The UDF was a staunch critic of all the homelands leaders whom they regarded as sell-outs. As links between the UDF and the ANC grew stronger, so UDF denunciations of Inkatha became more frequent. Inkatha opposed what it saw as an attempt by the ANC to turn the UDF from a broad-based front organization into an arm of the ANC, and as the UDF and the ANC grew closer together, so Zulu and Inkatha supporters withdrew from the UDF.

Conflicts also erupted between ANC/UDF supporters and Inkatha members in the urban townships in the PWV triangle. These conflicts were partly over the allocation of resources within black areas but also because traditional residents in these areas opposed Zulu migrant workers and attacked them. This process mobilized Zulus behind Inkatha for their own self-protection.

In Natal, Inkatha fought ANC/UDF supporters for what it saw as encroachment on its territory and for attacks on its members, which it perceived as an attempt to displace it from traditional Zulu areas. On account of the numerical dominance of the Zulus in Natal, the UDF usually came off worst in the clashes between the two factions, while in the Transvaal the ANC/UDF usually fared better. On other occasions, the PAC or the *totsis* (gangsters) would provide incidents between the two groups in order to encourage the interfactional fighting.

The ANC had an advantage in that it had more support from non-Xhosa tribes than Inkatha had from non-Zulu groups, and whereas in the 1970s most of the homeland leaders such as Matanzima in Transkei or Sebe in Ciskei attempted to restrict ANC activities, in the 1980s homelands leaders, such as Enos Mabuza of Kangwane, tended to offer sympathy to the ANC and its mission in exile.

As the rising tide of violence swept the African townships in the late 1980s, and as established order collapsed, so the struggle intensified for the de facto control of the blacks living there. Although many people had political sympathy for the ANC, there was a growing concern that many of the people who were seeking to make the townships ungovernable, as Oliver Tambo had called for, were simply using the anarchy for their own financial benefit. Even after the release of Nelson Mandela and the unbanning of the ANC, it seemed that the ANC leadership was not in a position to control the township militants.

As the 1980s progressed, the struggle between Zulu impis

and supporters of the ANC/UDF grew more intense. Both Buthelezi and Mandela realized the damage that such struggles did to the black cause and, despite goodwill and appeals from both men, the violence and the deaths continued.

Throughout the 1980s cycles of violence and killings swept the black townships. Initially, these outbreaks of violence began as anti-government protests but soon developed into a power struggle between the ANC and the Inkatha Freedom Party for control of the black urban areas. The factors that tended to stimulate violence was the creation of power vacuums within the townships. Once the security forces were no longer in control, it was then up to one of the black groups to step into the void. In some cases, this would be the ANC/UDF, in others Inkatha or in others still, it might be AZAPO or *totsis*.

In some cases, discredit would be brought on a party by the actions of some of its members. In the case of the Stompie Moketsi affair, some of the bodyguards of Mrs Winnie Mandela, the wife of Nelson Mandela, were convicted of torturing a young boy to death. Although blacks did not relish the SADF patrolling their areas, the behaviour of the ANC in some of the townships led to a backlash against it. The same process also happened to Inkatha in areas where their members misbehaved. In other cases, individuals found that they had to take sides for their own protection. Zulus would be attacked because they were Zulus and hence they would end up fighting for Inkatha as a means of self-defence. Likewise, Xhosas would be attacked for being Xhosas and they would join the ANC for self-protection. The cycles and spirals of violence inexorably drew people into groups often out of necessity and because people had no alternative to joining a group if they wished to survive.

The Churches, the UDF and COSATU

In the late 1970s and early 1980s with the major political movements, the ANC and the PAC banned, other groups emerged to fill the vacuum in black opposition politics inside South Africa. The Afrikaners thought of themselves as a religious people, and so it was always much harder for them to persecute ministers of the Christian Church, even the representatives of other Churches. This meant that clerics would often be able to make more strident denunciations of the National government in the knowledge that they would have a greater degree of safety than their secular counterparts.

The clergy therefore provided the nucleus of the leadership for local black communities. A number of the early leaders of the ANC were members of the Anglican clergy and Anglican clergy were to continue to play a prominent role in opposing racial discrimination throughout the twentieth century.

The influence of the Calvinist religion played an important role in the creation of the doctrine of apartheid. Apartheid was a world view that governed not only how relations should be between the citizen and God, but also the citizen and the Church, the citizen and the family, the family and the community and the relations between different communities.

The Dutch Reformed Church provided many recruits for the National Party, including many of its leading activists. The Church also gave the National Party's political platform a religious justification. If the links between the Afrikaners and their religion, which justified apartheid in biblical terms, were strong, so also were the links between the anti-apartheid groups and their Churches. Ultimately, in the 1980s, even the majority of the Calvinist Churches were to reject apartheid. Religious opposition to apartheid can be divided into those Churches which always opposed racial discrimination, those Churches which were associated with communities in South Africa other than the Afrikaners, and finally those Churches and churchmen within the Afrikaner community which came to break with apartheid.

One of the best known of the Calvinist Afrikaner clergy to break with apartheid was Dr Beyers Naude. Naude came from an impeccable Afrikaner background, but in the 1960s he found that he could no longer accept the apartheid interpretation of Christianity. He was to endure persecution by Vorster's Bureau of State Security for over a decade because of his opposition to apartheid. In the 1980s many more members of the Dutch Reformed Church were to follow his example.

The Anglican Church had many branches throughout the world and many of their congregations were in independent black states. From 1948 onwards they persistently condemned apartheid and through their links with the World Council of Churches gave aid to the African liberation movements in Namibia, Rhodesia and South Africa. Some members of the clergy such as Bishop Trevor Huddleston and Canon Collins were longstanding supporters of the anti-apartheid cause.

The Roman Catholic Church also became more critical of apartheid in the post-1945 era and its clergy took a more active role in opposing racial discrimination on a global basis.

There was a long history of independent black Churches going back to the nineteenth century, such as the African Methodist Episcopal Church. A certain amount of segregation occurred in Churches for geographic reasons but statutory attempts to enforce segregation were met with opposition from the clergy of most denominations.

Segregation in Churches, however, did have some benefits for blacks. It meant that the Churches could address other matters besides spiritual affairs. As successive National governments stepped up political repression, the Churches provided one arena of protest where that repression was less severe than elsewhere. Therefore it was no surprise that, with the black community's political élite either jailed or in exile, members of the black clergy should be prominent in organizing community action in the 1970s and should also be active in the UDF in the 1980s.

One cleric who was one of the most outspoken opponents of the National government in the 1970s and 1980s was the Anglican Archbishop Desmond Tutu. In 1984 Tutu was awarded the Nobel Peace Prize for his efforts to bring about reconciliation in South Africa. Tutu had consistently called for the release of Nelson Mandela and for dialogue between the government and the ANC. Tutu called for the implementation of sanctions against the South African government but regularly condemned the necklace killings that were carried out by ANC activists in the 1980s and 1990s.

The UDF was formed in 1983 as a result of a series of protests at Botha's new constitution. Many blacks felt that this constitution was going to disenfranchise them permanently, while there was fear among both the coloured and Asian communities that they dare not accept participation lest black fury be turned on them, a danger to which they might have become exposed without gaining any significant concessions in return from the whites. To many coloureds and Asians the 1983 constitution was a shameless piece of divide and rule strategy by the whites and one that actually offered them little.

The most prominent figure associated with the UDF is Dr

Allan Boesak. Dr Boesak was a leading figure in the World Alliance of Reformed Churches and within this forum he had vigorously denounced apartheid. The UDF was to remain a broad coalition of groups and it made clear that it was not going to become a political party. As a coalition, it retained advantages, whereas if it had become a party, it might well have been banned or suffered severe restrictions, such as those faced by the BPC in the 1970s. As a political body the UDF would have had either to oppose or support the ANC, in which latter case it would have invited legal persecution. By remaining a coalition, it could follow its political orientation towards the ANC without fear of reprisal.

In 1987 a number of UDF leaders flew to Lusaka to meet the ANC leadership in exile. For its part the ANC warmly welcomed the UDF and applauded its campaign of opposition to the Botha government. There was one issue on which the UDF and the ANC differed and that was the question of the use of violence. The UDF clearly stated that it was not going to use violence in order to further its objectives. If the UDF was to have declared its intention to use violence, then the full resources of the South African state would have been brought to bear against the organization and so destroyed its limited freedom of action.

In addition to its total rejection of the 1983 constitution, the UDF also declared its complete hostility to the homelands structures and their leaders, even Chief Buthelezi. The hostility between the UDF and Inkatha was caused in part by the ideological similarity of their views and in part by most of the UDF leadership's sympathy for Inkatha's rival the ANC. But both the UDF and Inkatha opposed violence and called for bridge-building with the white community. In Buthelezi's case, his proposals for the KwaZulu-Natal indaba were greeted with enthusiasm from most sections of the white community, although not by P.W. Botha or his supporters in the National Party.

However, Buthelezi retained a large amount of sympathy and tacit support among the white community, particularly in Natal, and he also had the advantage of good relations with the powerful conservative governments in Britain, Germany and the United States. The conservative governments which had dominated Britain, Germany and the United States in the 1980s remained highly suspicious of the ANC because of its extensive communist links.

Buthelezi had already secured allies among reformist whites, the very people whom the ANC and the UDF were hoping to win over. Many former ANC activists joined the UDF, thus increasing that organization's antipathy to Inkatha. The final break came when the UDF endorsed the ANC and became more stridently hostile towards Inkatha. UDF activists also began to protest against aspects of the KwaZulu administration and thus confronted Inkatha on its home ground. Although the UDF and Inkatha both publicly opposed the use of violence for political ends, in reality their members regularly engaged in pitched battles for the control of territory.

The UDF and the Congress of South African Trade Unions (COSATU) were both to benefit from the limited reforms of the late 1970s. COSATU was able to exploit greater opportunities in the sphere of labour relations as a result of the Wiehahn Commission. The UDF was able to engage in limited forms of political protest because Botha was under intense international pressure to pursue domestic reforms and he could hardly be seen to be attacking one of the few opposition groups that was still legal. However, with the unrest in the townships after 1984, the government arrested and detained many of the UDF leaders. It seemed that once again escalating protests were to be met with the predictable response of new security restrictions and tough action from the security forces.

Prospects for a Solution

Between 1948 and 1978 the majority of the white South African population was not interested in the rights of the country's black majority. From 1978 until 1989 P.W. Botha made a significant attempt to overturn the structures of apartheid. Yet for all Botha's attempts to formulate change, he was unsuccessful and his period in office saw an increase in South Africa's political isolation, a worsening economic performance and a deteriorating public order problem.

Botha's idea of a tricameral parliament had not worked. He did not win over enough coloureds and Asians and only succeeded in alienating the blacks. At the same time, it should be emphasized that Botha's reforms were a more dramatic advance on anything the National Party had done in over forty years. It was clear that by 1985 the black majority in South

Africa would not accept a racially divided parliament nor the idea that they should be deprived of South African citizenship in order to become citizens in the homelands. This meant that any attempt by the Botha government to try and use homeland structures as part of a future solution was doomed to fail.

For his part, Botha was faced by a number of constraints on how far he could make concessions without losing the support of his party and the majority of the white electorate. Meanwhile, a number of the exile groups believed that if they waited long enough, time was on their side so there was little point in trying to negotiate with Pretoria in the short or medium term.

There were also a number of obstacles to negotiations between the ANC and the government. These included the lifting of the state of emergency, the release of Mandela and other prisoners and the unbanning of the ANC and the other opposition groups. In return, the government wanted the ANC to abandon its campaign of armed struggle. It was left to Botha's successor, F. W. de Klerk, to take these steps.

De Klerk's administration faced a number of serious problems: first, the economy was in a shambles and desperately needed foreign investment, which was unlikely to be forthcoming while the cornerstones of apartheid remained in place; second, there was a growing cycle of violence between the two major black groups, the UDF/ANC and Inkatha, and the security forces seemed unable to contain this violence.

The key issues that would determine the future of South Africa were the future constitutional arrangements of the country, the question of parliamentary practice, the make-up of the future security forces and the economic strategy of a future government. If the whites were to concede the principle of majority rule, did that mean in an adversarial system such as the British parliament or did it mean some form of consociational democracy where the whites would always have some share of political office?

If the whites were to concede black majority rule, what guarantees would there be for whites by way of economic and employment security in the future? If a consociational arrangement was established between the National Party, the ANC and Inkatha, what would happen to groups such as the PAC and the Conservative Party, both of which were so opposed to the idea? Furthermore, how was the question of future sub-state violence to be dealt with as it was proving difficult enough to contain the war between the supporters of the ANC and Inkatha?

Perhaps the most serious long-term problem was the South African economy, and the need for that economy to provide sufficient new jobs for the growing black population in the early twenty-first century. Unemployment and poverty are often breeding grounds for discontent that in due course can be channelled into political opposition. If South Africa was going to be a harmonious society then clearly jobs would have to be created in order to keep pace with the rate of demographic increase.

In the 1990s external factors are extremely favourable for assisting in the peaceful resolution of the South African conflict. Between 1945 and 1985 southern Africa was seen in geopolitical terms by the NATO and Warsaw Pact blocs. The Americans and their allies saw South Africa as being important because of its mineral resources and its role in guarding the sea route round the Cape of Good Hope. Many whites, especially in Britain, had friends or family living in South Africa and many European companies had extensive business interests there. In time, the NATO countries came to distance themselves from Pretoria because of their opposition to the policies of apartheid.

The Soviet Union gave military aid to most of the national liberation movements in southern Africa and even established close ties with a number of the frontline states such as Angola. However, the military aid that the Soviet Union gave to both the frontline states and the liberation movement was not without obligations. First, the Soviet Union made some very tough trade deals with the African countries in which the Soviets gained much more than they lost. Second, the Soviet Union lacked the financial resources necessary for long-term investment in these countries and was unable to supply them with capital or management training. On the other hand, the NATO countries had an abundance of capital and plenty of technical expertise to give to the frontline states.

The Soviet Union faced more serious problems when anti-communist guerrilla forces began to mount extensive operations against Angola and Mozambique. This meant that the Soviet Union had to spend ever greater amounts of money to support its allies. This expenditure soon became a drain on Soviet resources and played an important part in reshaping

Soviet foreign policy in southern Africa. The domestic changes taking place in the Soviet Union under President Gorbachev's policies of *glasnost* and *perestroika* led to a considerable rethinking of Soviet-African policy.

From the mid-1980s, the Soviet Union began to look for compromise and conciliation with the United States rather than to pursue policies of confrontation and military adventurism. Such policies meant that southern Africa ceased to be regarded as a pawn in the Cold War and this proved to be of benefit to all parties. It helped towards creating the settlement that led to Namibian independence and it also led to increased Soviet pressure on the ANC to consider negotiations with the South African government and to increased pressure from the West on the South African government to negotiate with the ANC. The superpowers were able to make constructive contributions to solving the South African conflict because they had not only leverage on the major parties but also a willingness to seek a solution that would be beneficial to all parties.

Despite the many obstacles that lie in the way of a peaceful settlement to the conflict and all the problems involved in creating a society with the economic resources to sustain a decent standard of living for its citizens, southern Africa does have successful precedents for conflict resolution. The Boer Wars were bitterly contested but the English and the Boers became reconciled and served in government together. The Afrikaners sought to govern alone after 1948 but found that first they had to include non-Afrikaner whites in their ranks and then they had to include coloureds and Asians. In time not only will they have to come to terms with blacks but they will have to give up the power they have cherished for the major part of the twentieth century and accept that in the future they will only have a lesser role.

One of the central problems that has haunted the South African conflict has been the clash of nationalisms. British imperialism, Afrikaner nationalism and African nationalism: each of these nationalisms has found self-expression by denying the self-expression of the other nationalisms. British imperialism had no room for the Boers and a second-class position for blacks, Afrikaner nationalism had no place for the English and a subservient role for blacks, while African nationalism had no place for whites. In a future South Africa, nationalism will have to be defined in such a way that all people regardless of race will be able to identify with it: only then will there be a chance for a just and lasting peace.

It was clear in 1991 that the National Party, the ANC and Inkatha were all powerful forces but none of these groups was strong enough to govern without the consent or support of the others. Yet any of these three groups did have the capacity to wreck an agreement that did not suit them. Above all what is necessary for a peaceful resolution of the South African crisis is that each of these groups is committed to a solution that involves the other two parties. Although negotiations have still a long way to go, there is every indication that the leaderships of these groups are committed to such a solution.

APPENDIX A

PRIME MINISTERS AND STATE PRESIDENTS OF SOUTH AFRICA: 1910–91

Prime Ministers	Years in Office
L. Botha	1910–19
J.C. Smuts	1919–24
B. Hertzog	1924–39
J.C. Smuts	1939–48
D.F. Malan	1948–54
J.G. Strijdom	1954–58
H.F. Verwoerd	1958–66
B.J. Vorster	1966–78
P.W. Botha	1978–84

State President	Years in Office
P.W. Botha	1984–89
F.W. de Klerk	1989–

APPENDIX B

PUBLIC ADMINISTRATION IN SOUTH AFRICA UNDER P. W. BOTHA

Public administration in South Africa has undergone two major changes since 1945. After 1948 the National Party used the civil service to provide job security for its supporters. Many of these people were not well educated and had not the background for commerce. Until the Second World War the public service, and in particular its upper echelons, was dominated by English-speakers. Malan and his successors began to replace many of the senior civil service officials with Afrikaners until by the 1960s both the SADF and the civil service were dominated by them. The many apartheid laws and regulations required a bureaucracy of clerks to implement and monitor and it was the Afrikaners who made up the majority of the staff administering black affairs. This was to give many poor whites a vested interest in the maintenance of apartheid. In many other African countries, new élites, on taking power, would promptly use the civil service to provide jobs for their supporters and to ensure that their bureaucracy was politically reliable. Many whites feared that in the event of black majority rule, a future black government would do the same, thus throwing the poor whites out of their jobs. As both Pottinger, in his assessment of the Botha era entitled *The Imperial Presidency*, and Wassenaar in *En Route To Fairyland*, pointed out, the Afrikaner civil servants have done exceptionally well out of the Nationl Party and their living standards and pension entitlements are much higher than any comparable state with the same per capita income. Clearly, whatever the future held for the Afrikaner civil service, they could not expect the benefits that they had received in the past to continue indefinitely.

P. W. Botha had served most of his time in cabinet as the Defence Minister and so had considerable experience of the civil service bureaucracy. Civil service practice under the National government had not always been efficient. Cabinet minutes were not taken regularly until the 1950s and the bureaucracy had expanded with many overlapping functions. Botha intended to change all that.

Botha's plan of reform was partly for political and partly for administrative reasons. He wished to increase the role of the Department of Defence as it had been his power base and he wished to reduce the role of BOSS and the South African police, which had been under the control of his rivals. Botha had also instituted a number of administrative reforms in the Department of Defence which had improved its economy, effectiveness and efficiency. These measures included improving the quality of senior managers within the civil service, reducing the number of ministerial departments and setting up a centralized military planning system. It was in the military arena that pay differentials between the racial groups was first substantially diminished, as was the psychologically important step of putting blacks in senior positions to whites. Botha's experience of running the Department of Defence led him to institute similar reforms in others areas of the public sector, once he became Prime Minister.

In 1978 under Vorster, South Africa had thirty-nine ministerial departments and over twenty cabinet committees, which frequently carried out similar functions. Initially, Botha reduced the bureaucracy to twenty-two departments and four main committees. The main committees were, most importantly, the State Security Council (SCC), the Economic Affairs Committee, the Social Affairs Committee and the Internal Affairs Committee. Each of these committees met regularly and was interlinked to the Prime Minister's office via a planning branch. Ironically, the number of ministerial positions was to expand during the 1980s once coloured and Asian ministers were appointed to service their own affairs.

The most important cabinet committee was the SSC. Its members included: the Prime Minister (P. W. Botha), the Minister for the Department of Defence (Magnus Malan), the Minister for the Department of Foreign Affairs (R. F. 'Pik' Botha), the Minister for Law and Order (initially Louis Le Grange but later Adrian Vlok), and the Head of the National Intelligence Service (Professor L. D. Barnard). The State Security Council was at the top of a pyramid called the National Security Management System (NSMS), which contained a number of interlocking committees both at the central and local government level. These committees were organized on a regional level and were called Joint Management Centres. They comprised members of both local government and the local military and police leaders. They were designed to take proactive measures that would obviate any legitimate grievances on the part of the black community before local resentment led to serious rioting or actions by MK or APLA.

In 1981 the President's Council was created in an attempt to bring non-whites into the higher echelons of the decision-making process. The members of this body were nominated by the government, which provided a legitimacy problem for the coloureds and Asians who served on it. Both the coloured and Asian chambers in the tricameral parliament were elected on such a low turn-out at the polls that their legitimacy was severely questioned by the populations that they claimed to represent. Both the coloured and Asian populations rejected the previous nominated consultative bodies that were set up to speak for them on the grounds that the representatives were sell-outs. This problem also affected the administration of black areas.

Although some of the homeland leaders such as Buthelezi clearly had substantial popular support, the majority of such élites were regarded as sell-outs by the black population. Any nominal form of assembly within most homeland structures was so weighted down with appointees rather than representatives elected by the people that few homeland administrations enjoyed any popular support. Most homeland administrations were so dependent on Pretoria for financial assistance that it appeared that its members were simply the paid stooges of the National Party and hence collaborators in the implementation of apartheid.

Under the Bantu Homelands Citizenship Act of 1970, blacks were declared to have full rights within their homelands, which was seen by the National Party as a justification for depriving them of political, social and economic rights within 'white' South Africa. Yet substantial numbers of blacks continued to live in the townships, such as Soweto, near the 'white' heartlands. Furthermore, it was clear that the needs of the economy and of domestic service meant that it was simply not viable to use only migrant black labour.

From 1962 to 1977, Urban Bantu Councils were appointed to run the black areas, but their members were chosen by the Department of Co-operation and Development. These bodies were again seen as sell-outs by the majority of their populations and were a regular target of violence during township unrest, particularly during the 1976 Soweto uprising. After 1977, the government made these councils elected bodies but they still lacked adequate resources to run the townships and in too many cases were still seen to be puppets of the white administration. Local councillors continued to be targets for mob violence after 1984 along with black policemen.

APPENDIX C
THE MEDIA IN SOUTH AFRICA

For many years, the media in South Africa referred only to newspapers and magazines. It was only in 1976 that television was first licensed. The South African Broadcasting Corporation (SABC) was on air for a few hours each day but gradually its service was extended in line with public demand. In addition to television, the SABC was also responsible for a number of English and Afrikaans radio stations. Commercial advertising was permitted on all television channels. A number of radio programmes were carried in African languages as was a limited amount of material on television. The SABC traditionally took a pro-government position in its current affairs coverage and although in general it adopted a position supportive of the Botha government, there were still some serious disagreements between senior SABC officials and members of the Botha administration. In the last days of Botha's presidency and under de Klerk's administration, the corporation began to take a more independent position on matters of current affairs.

The South African press carried the burden of strict censorship laws that governed their coverage of political protest and all matters pertaining to national security. Under the Defence Act of 1957, newspapers were prohibited from discussing the movements or strengths of the South African Defence Force. This meant that the South African press were unable to publish accounts of the SADF incursion into Angola in 1976, although the information was available to the public from external sources. The South African public were informed of the SADF involvement in the Angolan civil war through radio broadcasts, foreign newspapers that were smuggled into the country and from South Africans who either lived or travelled abroad. Other public order legislation prevented the press from covering demonstrations, rioting or other forms of protest.

As the 1980s progressed and the government talked about ending apartheid, a number of leading journalists took a prominent role in publicly exploring future policy options for sharing power with the black population. Yet once they had grasped the nettle of reform, many of these leading Afrikaners became impatient with the government's lack of negotiation with any of the major black groups. In 1988 Harold Pakendorf, editor of *Die Vaderland*, and Willem de Klerk, editor of *Rapport*, both left their jobs, condemning the government for being too preoccupied with security and not doing enough by way of political negotiation. De Klerk, the brother of F. W de Klerk the future State President, argued that he was under too much pressure to give a National Party perspective in the paper's coverage.

Ironically, criticisms of the Afrikaans press were levelled from both the right as well as the left. In 1983, the Afrikaans press refused adverts from the pro-apartheid Conservative Party as well as from the reformist Progressive Federal Party on the issue of the referendum on Botha's new constitution. The Conservative Party campaigned for a no-vote because they were opposed to any form of power-sharing with other racial groups, while the Progressives were opposed to the new constitution because it offered nothing to the blacks.

However, such restrictions did not prevent the press from exposing major government corruption scandals, such as the Information affair. Many South African journalists, such as Mervyn Rees, Chris Day, Fleur de Villiers, Hennie Serfontein, Brian Pottinger, Donald Woods and Harold Pakendorf, achieved international reputations for the high quality of their work. Black journalists suffered under much greater handicaps than whites. Their scope for political comment was severely limited until the presidency of F.W. de Klerk and a large number of black journalists were prosecuted for violations of security restrictions. Perhaps the black journalist who was best known outside South Africa was the late Percy Qoboza, the editor of the *World*.

Donald Woods was editor of the *Daily Dispatch* and gave prominent coverage to the views of black politicians in the 1970s within the limits of the strict security laws. Woods became friendly with Steve Biko, leader of the Black Consciousness Movement, and exposed the brutal manner of Biko's death in police detention; he was himself banned for this disclosure and for his criticism of government policy. After several years of continued harassment, Woods and his family escaped from South Africa to live in exile in Britain. After 1989 the political climate became more tolerant and in due course Woods and a number of other journalists returned to South Africa.

The English newspapers have traditionally been critical of Nationalist governments and have often been subjected to greater attack under the various press restrictions. One reason for this is that many blacks prefer to read the English press because it is superior in quality to the Afrikaans papers. The English press is much older than the Afrikaans, some of the newspapers going back to the middle of the nineteenth century, whereas the major Afrikaans papers really only achieved prominence after the First World War. There are two major English publishing houses, the Argus group and the South African Associated Newspapers group (SAAN). The Argus group owns two important daily papers, the *Johannesburg Star* and the *Cape Town Argus*. The SAAN group owned the *Rand Daily Mail* (until it was closed down), the *Financial Mail* and the *Johannesburg Sunday Times*. The English press captures around 75 per cent of the market for daily newspapers and over 50 per cent of the weekly press.

The two major Afrikaans press groups are Perskor and Nasionale Pers. The Perskor group owns the influential Johannesburg dailies

Die Transvaaler and *Die Vaderland*, although both groups had sizeable stakes in *Rapport*. Nasionale Pers owns *Die Burger*, the main Afrikaans daily paper in the Cape Town area.

ABBREVIATIONS AND GLOSSARY OF
POLITICAL TERMS

ANC—African National Congress, the main African opposition group. President, Oliver Tambo; Vice-President, Nelson Mandela.

APLA—Anzanian People's Liberation Army, military wing of the PAC. It was formerly known as Poqo.

ARMSCOR—Armaments Corporation of South Africa, parastatal organization aimed at acquiring or developing weapons and munitions for the SADF.

AWB—Afrikaner Weerstandsbeweging, Afrikaner Resistance Movement led by Eugene Terreblanche.

AZAPO—Azanian People's Organization, heir of the Black Consciousness Movement, closely allied to the PAC.

Black Consciousness Movement (BCM)—Community-based movement in the 1970s led by Steve Biko.

Black People's Convention (BPC)—One of the main groups associated with the Black Consciousness Movement.

BOSS—Bureau of State Security, the South African intelligence agency, headed by General H. J. van den Bergh. Reorganized after the Information scandal and became the Department of National Security.

Broederbond—Secret society, founded by Henning Klopper, dedicated to ensuring Afrikaners keep control of the important positions in government, industry and the armed forces.

CIO—Central Intelligence Organization, Rhodesian secret intelligence organization headed by Ken Flower.

Conservative Party—Formed in 1982 by breakaway members of the National Party, led by Dr A. Treurnicht.

COREMO—Mozambican Resistance Committee, anti-Portuguese and anti-Frelimo group, active prior to 1975. A number of their members subsequently joined Renamo.

COSATU—Congress of South African Trade Unions, largest of the black trade union federations.

CUSA—Council of Unions of South Africa.

DMI—Department of Military Intelligence, one of the most powerful branches of the military, that was to become more prominent after 1979, taking over a number of functions from BOSS.

DTA—Democratic Turnhalle Alliance, anti-SWAPO coalition in Namibia. Most prominent leader Dirk Mudge.

FAK—Federasie van Afrikaanse Kultuuvereniginge, Afrikaner cultural organization that played an important role in the development of the Afrikaner nationalist movement in the 1930s.

FNLA—National Front for the Liberation of Angola, pro-Western Angolan movement opposed to the Marxist MPLA. The FNLA is based in the north of the country and is led by Holden Roberto.

140

FOSATU—Federation of South African Trade Unions.

Frelimo—Front for the Liberation of Mozambique, the governing party in Mozambique, which came to power following the Portuguese withdrawal. Led by Eduardo Mondlane until his assassination, then by Samora Machel, until his death in a plane crash in 1986. Current leader is Joaquim Chissano.

HNP—Herstigte National Party, right-wing opposition party led by Jaap Marais.

Inkatha—Zulu-based opposition party led by Chief Gatsha Buthelezi.

ISCOR—Iron and Steel Corporation.

Labour Party—The main political party in the Coloured House of Representatives led by Reverend Allan Hendrikse.

MNR—Mozambique National Resistance, also known as Renamo.

MPLA—The People's Movement for the Liberation of Angola.

MWU—Mine Workers Union, white union opposed to reforms that erode apartheid.

National Party—The major party representing white Afrikaners since 1945 which has been continuously in government since 1948.

NGK—Nederduitse Gereformeerde Kerk, the Dutch Reformed Church.

NIS—National Intelligence Service, formerly the Department of National Security headed by Dr L. D. Barnard.

PAC—Pan-Africanist Congress, the organization led by Robert Sobukwe and Potlake Leballo, which opposed non-blacks having a major role in the anti-apartheid struggle.

PFP—Progressive Federal Party, the major white liberal opposition party, which draws most of its support from the English-speakers.

Poqo—Military wing of the PAC. It was subsequently renamed the APLA.

President's Council—This was an advisory body established in 1981.

Renamo—Mozambican National Resistance Movement, anti-communist guerrilla force dedicated to the overthrow of the Frelimo government.

Rhodesia Front—White party that ruled Rhodesia for most of the period between 1965 and 1980, led by Ian Smith.

SABC—South African Broadcasting Corporation, state-run television and radio service.

SABRA—South African Bureau of Racial Affairs.

SACP—South African Communist Party.

SACTU—South African Council of Trade Unions.

SADCC—South African Development Co-ordinating Council. Formed by Angola, Botswana, Lesotho, Malawi, Mozambique, Swaziland, Tanzania, Zambia and Zimbabwe in order to reduce their economic and material dependence on South Africa.

SADF—South African Defence Force. It refers collectively to the army, navy, air force and the medical service.

SAP—South African Police.

SASO—South African Students Organization. A break-away group from the multiracial National Union of South African Students formed by Steve Biko.

Securocrats—A term used to describe the military advisers of P. W. Botha.

Selous Scouts—Élite Rhodesian special forces unit, commanded by Lt-Colonel Ron Reid-Daly.

SWAPO—South-West Africa People's Organization. The Namibian national-liberation movement, led by Sam Nujoma, it formed the first government in independent Namibia.

Swart Gevaar—Black peril. A term used to describe white fears of a black takeover.

Total Onslaught—A term used by the 'securocrats' to describe what they perceived to be a combined external and internal threat to the white community in South Africa.

Total Strategy—An all-embracing strategy designed by the 'securocrats' to counter total onslaught.

TUCSA—Trade Union Congress of South Africa.

UCOR—Uranium Corporation of South Africa.

UDF—United Democratic Front (formed in 1983), anti-apartheid protest movement closely aligned to the ANC.

UNITA—National Union for the Total Independence of Angola. Anti-communist guerrilla force, it is supported by the largest ethnic group in Angola, the Ovimbundu. It was founded and continues to be led by Jonas Savimbi.

UWUSA—United Workers Union of South Africa, Zulu-based trade union group formed because of Zulu protest at COSATU alignment with the UDF and the ANC.

ZANLA—Zimbabwean African National Liberation Army, military wing of ZANU (PF).

ZANU—Party led by Reverend Ndabaningi Sithole. The party joined the coalition government led by Bishop Abel Muzorewa but was decimated in the pre-independence elections.

ZANU (PF)—Political party led by Robert Mugabe and supported by the Shona speakers in Rhodesia. PF signifies that this party was part of the Patriotic Front, the guerrilla coalition that was opposed to white rule in Rhodesia. ZANU has been the governing party in Zimbabwe since independence.

ZAPU—Zimbabwean African Political Union, led by Joshua Nkomo, it drew its support from the Ndebele tribe in south-western Rhodesia.

ZIPRA—Independent People's Revolutionary Army of Zimbabwe, guerrilla force loyal to Joshua Nkomo, military wing of ZAPU.

BIBLIOGRAPHY

General

L.J. Boulle—*South Africa: The Consociational Option* (Johannesburg: Juta, 1984)

P. Collins—*Thinking About South Africa* (Hemel Hempstead: Harvester, 1990)

V. Crapanzano—*Waiting: The Whites of South Africa* (London: Granada, 1985)

T. Davenport—*A History of South Africa* (London: Macmillan, 1977)

A. DuPisani—*United or Divided Power* (Johannesburg: Lex Patria, 1986)

L.H. Gann and P. Duignan—*South Africa: War, Revolution or Peace* (Stanford: Hoover Institution Press, 1979).

K. Ingham—*Jan Christian Smuts* (London: Weidenfeld & Nicolson, 1986)

W. James—*The State of Apartheid* (Boulder, Colorado: Lyne Reiner, 1987)

S. Johnston—*South Africa: No Turning Back* (London: Macmillan, 1988)

G. Leach—*South Africa* (London: Century Hutchinson, 1986)

G. Leach—*The Afrikaners* (London: Macmillan, 1989)

M. Meredith—*In the Name of Apartheid* (London: Hamish Hamilton, 1988)

B. Pottinger—*The Imperial Presidency* (Johannesburg: Southern, 1988)

A. Prior and L. Thompson—*South African Politics* (New Haven: Yale University Press, 1982)

D. Venter—*The Government and Politics of South Africa* (Johannesburg: Southern, 1988)

Defence and Foreign Affairs

J. Barber—*The Uneasy Relationship: British Policy Towards South Africa* (London: Heinemann Educational Books, 1983)

J. Barber and J. Barratt—*South African Foreign Policy* (Cambridge: Cambridge University Press, 1990)

F. Bridgland—*Jonas Savimbi* (Edinburgh: Mainstream, 1986)

C. Coker—*NATO, The Warsaw Pact and Africa* (London: Macmillan, 1986)

P. Frankel—*Pretoria's Praetorians* (Cambridge: Cambridge University Press, 1984)

D. Geldenhuys—*The Diplomacy of Isolation* (London: Macmillan, 1984)

K. Grundy—*The Militarisation of South African Politics* (London: I.B. Tauris, 1986)

J. Hanlon—*Beggar Your Neighbours* (London: James Currey, 1986)

H.R. Heitman—*The South African War Machine* (Bromley: Cщago, 1985)

J. Heunis—*United Nations and South Africa* (Johannesburg: Lex Patria, 1987)

R. Jackson—*Security: A National Strategy* (Johannesburg: Lex Patria, 1987)

R. Jaster—*The Defence of White Power* (London: Macmillan, 1988)

R. Jaster—*South Africa In Namibia* (Lanham, Maryland: University Press of America, 1985)

S. Landgren—*Embargo Disemplemented* (Oxford: Oxford University Press, 1989)

R. Leonard—*South Africa at War* (Westport, Connecticut: Lawrence Hill, 1983)

J. Moore—*South Africa and Nuclear Proliferation* (London: Macmillan, 1986)

W. Steenkamp—*Borderstrike: South Africa into Angola* (Durban: Butterworth, 1983)

The Opposition

M. Benson—*Nelson Mandela* (Harmondsworth: Penguin, 1986)

S. Boulay—*Tutu: Voice of the Voiceless* (London: Hodder & Stoughton, 1988)

B. Breytenbach—*Confessions of an Albino Terrorist* (London: Faber & Faber, 1984)

S. Davis—*Apartheid's Rebels* (New Haven: Yale University Press, 1987)

B. Hirson—*Year of Fire, Year of Ash* (London: Zed Press, 1979)

H. Holland—*The Struggle* (London: Grafton, 1989)

D.J. Kotze—*African Politics and South Africa* (London: Charles Hurst, 1975)

D.J. Kotze—*Communism and South Africa* (Cape Town: Tafelberg, 1979)

T. Lodge *Black Politics in South Africa* (Harlow: Longman, 1983)

A. Luthuli—*Let My People Go* (London: Fount, 1982)

G. Mare and G. Hamilton—*An Appetite for Power: Buthelezi's Inkatha and South Africa* (Braamfontein: Ravan Press, 1987)

A. Tambo—*Oliver Tambo Speaks* (London: Heinemann, 1987)

D. Tutu—*Hope and Suffering* (Johannesburg: Skotaville, 1984)

D. Woods—*Biko* (London: Penguin, 1979)

Economic and Social Policy

H. Adam and K. Moodley—*South Africa Without Apartheid* (Berkeley: University of California Press, 1986)

D. Austin—*South Africa 1984* (London: Routledge & Kegan Paul/Royal Institute of International Affairs, 1985)

J. Barber, J. Blumenfeld and C. Hill—*The West and South Africa* (London: Routledge & Kegan Paul/Royal Institute of International Affairs, 1982)

J. Blumenfeld (ed)—*South Africa In Crisis* (Beckenham: Croon Helm, 1987)

K.H. Butts and P.R. Thomas—*The Geopolitics of Southern Africa* (Boulder, Colorado: Westview Press, 1986)

K. Costa—*An African Affair* (London: Centre For Policy Studies, 1990)

H. Giliomee and L. Schlemmer—*Up Against the Fences* (New York: St Martins Press, 1984)

H. Giliomee and L. Schlemmer—*From Apartheid to Nation-Building* (Oxford: Oxford University Press, 1989)

H. Giliomee and L. Schlemmer—*Negotiating South Africa's Future* (Johannesburg: Southern, 1989)

T. Green—*The New World of Gold* (London: Weidenfeld & Nicolson, 1981)

W. Gutteridge—*Mineral Resources and National Security* (London: Institute for the Study of Conflict, 1984)

W. Gutteridge—*The South African Crisis: Time for International Action* (London: Institute for the Study of Conflict, 1985)

D. Innes—*Anglo-American and the Rise of Modern South Africa* (London: Heinemann, 1984)

M. Johns—*U.S. and Africa Statistical Handbook* (Washington: The Heritage Foundation, 1991)

M. Lipton—*Capitalism and Apartheid* (London: Gower, 1985)

J. Marcum—*Education, Race and Change in South Africa* (Berkeley, California: University of California Press, 1982)

D. Pallister, S. Stewart and I. Lepper—*South Africa Inc: The Oppenheimer Empire* (London: Simon & Schuster, 1987)

A. Rupert—*Priorities for Coexistence* (Cape Town: Tafelberg, 1981)

A. Sampson—*Black and Gold* (London: Hodder & Stoughton, 1987)

D. Smith—*Living Under Apartheid* (London: Allen & Unwin, 1982)

C. Sunter—*The World and South Africa in the 1990s* (Cape Town: Tafelberg, 1987)

D. Van Vuren et al—*South Africa: A Plural Society in Transition* (Durban: Butterworth, 1985)

A.D. Wassenaar—*Assault On Private Enterprise* (Cape Town: Tafelberg, 1977)

A.D. Wassenaar—*En Route to Fairyland* (Cape Town: Tafelberg, 1987)

CHRONOLOGY OF RECENT EVENTS: 1976–91

1976—Popular uprising in the black township of Soweto, near Johannesburg, following the government's introduction of Afrikaans as the medium of instruction in black schools.

1977—Steve Biko, leader of the Black Consciousness Movement, dies in police custody. United Nations announces a mandatory arms embargo against South Africa.

1978—Prime Minister B.J. Vorster resigns and becomes State President. P.W. Botha becomes Prime Minister. The SADF launches Operation Reindeer to attack SWAPO bases in southern Angola.

1979—The publication of the last section of the Erasmus Report into the Information scandal states that former Prime Minister B.J. Vorster was aware of financial irregularities in the Department of Information. The SADF attack southern Angola and Zambia as a response to SWAPO actions in Namibia.

1980—Elections held in Rhodesia–Zimbabwe give Robert Mugabe, leader of ZANU (PF), an overwhelming majority. Rhodesia–Zimbabwe becomes Zimbabwe and Robert Mugabe becomes Prime Minister. Angola, Botswana, Lesotho, Malawi, Mozambique, Tanzania, Swaziland, Zambia and Zimbabwe form the SADCC in an attempt to lessen economic dependence on South Africa. The SADF again launches a major land and air assault into southern Angola to attack SWAPO bases.

1981—The SADF launch Operation Protea to attack SWAPO bases in Angola. Lt-Col Ron Reid-Daly, former commanding officer of the Rhodesian Selous Scouts, becomes commander of the Transkei Defence Force. SADF special forces attack ANC supporters in Maseru, Lesotho.

1982—Cyril Ramaphosa and others launch the National Union of Mineworkers, which soon becomes one of the most powerful black unions. SADF special forces attack ANC buildings in Maseru, Lesotho, killing forty-two civilians. Formation of the Conservative Party, led by Dr Andries Treurnicht.

1983—P.W. Botha announces a new constitution and receives the support of 66 per cent of the white voters in a referendum. A car bomb in Pretoria, planted by the ANC, kills nineteen and injures 200. The SADF repeatedly strikes at ANC targets in Mozambique. The UDF is formed. Violence occurs between supporters of the UDF and Inkatha in Natal.

1984—P.W. Botha tours Europe to outline his plans for change in South Africa. He is warmly received in Britain and Germany. The South African and Angolan governments meet in Lusaka. Both countries agree to stop supporting guerrilla forces in each other's country. Facing domestic economic collapse and with anti-government guerrillas gaining popular support, Mozambican President Samora Machel signs the Nkomati Accord with South Africa. Major outbreaks of unrest occur in the black townships in protest at the new constitution.

1985—Violence erupts at the Crossroads squatter camp, near Cape Town. The conflict is fought out between vigilantes, known as the fathers, and younger radicals, known as the comrades. SADF special forces are caught trying to blow up oil depots in Cabinda, Angola. Over 2000 members of the AWB under Eugene Terreblanche march on Pretoria to protest at government concessions to blacks and at lack of sufficiently tough action to crush the protests in the townships. Serious rioting follows the shooting of a number of black civilians by the security forces in Uitenhage. ANC conference at Kabwe calls for a people's war. With a rising tide of violence in the townships, a state of emergency is declared and the government adopts new and tougher security legislation.

1986—Visit to South Africa by the Commonwealth Eminent Persons Group. The SADF attacks ANC targets in Gaberonne, Botswana. The government extends emergency legislation. During the next three years, over 20 000 people are held under the new laws passed under the state of emergency. ANC president Oliver Tambo meets British Minister of State at the Foreign Office, Mrs Linda Chalker, in London.

1987—Leading Afrikaner academics meet leaders of the ANC in Dakar, Senegal. Chief Jonathan of Lesotho is overthrown in a military coup by General Lekyana. The Soviet Union and Cuba mount major resupply missions to Angola and the Cuban troop numbers rise to 60 000. Reverend Allan Hendrickse, leader of the Coloured Labour Party, resigns from the government. Brigadier Holomisa of the Transkeian Defence force overthrows Kaiser Matanzima in a military coup.

1988—Dr Willem de Klerk resigns as managing editor of *Rapport*, the pro-government Afrikaans Sunday newspaper. South African intelligence assassinates ANC activist Dulcie September in France. Attempted coup in Bophuthatswana, the SADF intervenes to restore the Mangope government. Tripartite agreement signed between Cuba, Angola and South Africa, aimed at securing Namibian independence and the end to the presence of Cuban troops in Angola.

1989—P. W. Botha, suffering from ill-health, resigns as State President. F. W. de Klerk becomes the new leader of the National Party. De Klerk becomes State President and announces plans for reforms.

1990—President de Klerk releases veteran ANC leader Nelson Mandela and rescinds the ban on the ANC and the PAC. Violence continues between members of the ANC and Inkatha in both the Transvaal and Natal. It is estimated that over 2000 people have been killed in feuding between the ANC and Inkatha. Namibia becomes independent and SWAPO forms the first government.

1991—Nelson Mandela meets Chief Buthelezi in an attempt to halt the growing violence between the members of the ANC and Inkatha. The ANC held its first conference in South Africa for over thirty years in Durban, Natal. Attempts by Nelson Mandela to pursue a more pragmatic line in negotiations with both the National Party and Inkatha received a mixed reception from delegates. Mandela was elected President of the ANC and Cyril Ramaphosa, the leader of the National Union of Mineworkers, emerged as a powerful figure among the new generation of ANC leaders. The conference saw substantial disagreement among the ANC about both future strategy and policy. The divisions seemed to be concentrated between the hardline communists and the liberals, this division was echoed in the division between the members of MK and the political activists in the organization. President de Klerk paid a state visit to Kenya. In May 1991 the former British Prime Minister Margaret Thatcher visited South Africa. In June the MPLA and UNITA signed the Estoril accord, ending the sixteen-year-old Angolan civil war. The accord allowed the exchange of prisoners and for the introduction of free multiparty elections in 1992. The accord followed negotiations with the United Nations, Portugal, the United States and the Soviet Union. In July, South Africa was readmitted to international sport, and was granted permission to participate in the 1992 Olympic Games in Barcelona. This measure was greeted warmly by South African cricketing and athletics bodies and was seen as a particular vindication of the policies of multiracial integration pursued by Dr Ali Bacher. In the United States, President George Bush announced the lifting of most of the sanctions against South Africa imposed under the Comprehensive Anti-Apartheid Act (1986). Although Britain had already lifted many sanctions, the United Nations sanctions forbidding the sale of military weapons remained in place. In Europe, both the French and the Germans lifted a number of sanctions against South Africa in response to the reforms of President de Klerk. In the Far East, Japan followed suit, however, a number of governments declined to ease sanctions and among these were Canada.

INDEX

A

AAC (Anglo-American Corporation), 77,78, 80,81
ANC (African National Congress), 21,24,45, 50,52,66,70,91,92,93,94,98,100,101,104, 105,106,107,108,109,114,115,116,117, 119,120,121,122,123,124,125,126,127, 128,129,132
Angola, 41,42,43,44,45,46,47,50,51,52,53, 56,57,60,67,68,69,70,86,91,92,116
APLA (Azanian People's Liberation Army), 114
ARMSCOR (Armaments Corporation of South Africa), 53,95
AWB (Afrikaner Resistance Movement), 29
AZACTU (Azanian Confederation of Trade Unions), 102
AZAPO (Azanian People's Organization), 98, 120,124

B

Bacher, Dr Ali, 97
Banda, Dr Hastings, 47
Barayi, Elijah, 102
BCM (Black Consciousness Movement), 86, 98,118,119,120
Biko, Steve, 22,25,118,119,120
Boesak, Dr Allan, 126,127
Boshoff, Dr Carel, 32
BOSS (Bureau of State Security), 26,27,42
Botha, General Louis, 9,10
Botha, P. W., 25,26,27,29,30,36,37,38,50,54, 56,57,62,70,79,80,127,128,129
Botha, R. F. 'Pik', 25,37,38,42
BPC (Black People's Convention), 118,119
Broederbond, 14,32,40
Budd, Zola, 96,97
Buthelezi, Chief M.G., 22,28,120,121,122, 123,124,128

C

Caetano, Dr Marcelo, 42
Carrington, Lord, 49
Carter, President Jimmy, 46
CIA (Central Intelligence Agency), 44
CIO (Central Intelligence Organization), 45, 50
Ciskei, 22,76,123
Collins, Canon John, 126
Conservative Party (British), 49,94,97,127
Conservative Party (South African), 30,31, 32,33,34,72,73,100
COREMO (Mozambican Resistance Committee), 113

C (continued)

COSATU (Congress of South African Trade Unions), 102,103,104,124,128
Crocker, Dr Chester, 56
CYL (Congress Youth League), 106

D

De Beers, 77,80,81,82,83
de Klerk, F. W., 29,32,37,38,54,56,129
DMI (Department of Military Intelligence), 27
D'Oliveira, Basil, 96,97
Dube, Dr John, 105
Duncan, Sir Patrick, 13
Duncan, Patrick, 111
DTA (Democratic Turnhalle Alliance), 55,56

E

Eglin, Colin, 34
Erasmus, Judge, 26
ESCOM (Electricity Supply Commission), 84,85

F

FAK (Federation of Afrikaans Cultural Organizations), 13
Flower, Kenneth, 45,50
FNLA (National Front for the Liberation of Angola), 41,43,44,45,113
FOSATU (Federation of South African Trade Unions), 102
Frelimo (Front for the Liberation of Mozambique), 41,52,113,116

G

Gatting, Mike, 97
Gandhi, M.K., 104,108
Gorbachev, Mikhail, 131
Greig, Tony, 97
Group Areas Act (1950), 17,27,32

H

Hani, Chris, 118
Hertzog, Albert, 23,30
Hertzog, J.B.M., 10,11,12,13,15
Heunis, J.C., 36,37,38
HNP (Restructured National Party), 23,30
Hofmeyr, Jan, 11,16
Huddleston, Bishop Trevor, 111,126

I

Inkatha, 6,22,28,70,117,120,121,122,123, 124,127,128,129,130,132

Index

K

Kadalie, Clemens, 105
Kaunda, Dr Kenneth, 38,88
Klopper, Henning, 40

L

Leballo, Potlake, 111,113
Lembede, Anton, 106,107
Luthuli, Chief Albert, 108,109,121

M

Mabuza, Enos, 123
Machel, Samora, 70
MacMillan, Harold, 19,20,39,40
Make, Vus, 113
Malan, D.F., 1,13,14,15,16,17,18,79
Malan, General Magnus, 37,38,50
Mandela, Nelson, 21,38,91,106,107,110,123,
   124,126,129
Mandela, Winnie, 124
Matanzima, Kaiser, 22,123
Mbeki, Govan, 21,110
Milner, Lord Alfred, 9
MK, 67,110,115,117,118,121
Mlambo, Johnson, 114
MNR (Mozambique National Resistance), 51,
   52,53,64,66,92,113
Modise, Joe, 118
Moketsi, Stompie, 124
Moroka, Dr James, 105
Mostert Commission, 26
Mozambique, 6,7,41,42,45,47,70,88,101,113,
   116,117,122,130
MPLA (Popular Movement for the Liberation
   of Angola), 41,43,44,45,50,70,113,116
Mugabe, Robert, 48,49,50,87,88
Mulder, Dr Connie, 25,26
Muzorewa, Bishop Abel, 48,49
MWU (Mine Workers Union), 99

N

Naidoo, Jay, 102
Namibia, 27,42,46,50,53,54,55,56,57,69,124
National Forum, 120
National Party, 13,14,18,19,21,23,25,26,30,
   31,34,35,38,72,73,79,92,122,124,128
NATO (North Atlantic Treaty Alliance), 64,
   65,130
Naude, Dr Beyers, 124
Neto, Agostinho, 41
NIS (National Intelligence Service), 57
Nkomo, Joshua, 48,49,50

O

Oppenheimer, Ernest, 77,81,89
Oppenheimer, Harry, 77,79
Oppenheimer, Louis, 77

Oppenheimer, Nicholas, 79
Ossewa Brandweg, 14,21

P

PAC (Pan-Africanist Congress), 2,21,38,104,
   107,109,110,111,112,113,114,118,119,
   124
PFP (Progressive Federal Party), 34,35,36
Pityana, Barney, 118
Pokela, John, 113,114
Poqo, 112,114

R

Ramaphosa, Cyril, 103
Reagan, President Ronald, 97
Relly, Gavin, 79
Renamo (*see also* MNR), 51,53,70,88
Rhodesia, 22,24,40,41,45,47,48,49,50,69,90,
   91,113,124
Roberto, Holden, 41
Roux, Dr A.J., 85

S

SACOL (South African Confederation of
   Labour), 102
SACP (South African Communist Party), 2,
   38,42,86,106
SADCC (South African Development
   Co-ordinating Council), 70
SADF (South African Defence Force), 52,
   57,58,59,60,61,62,63,65,66,67
SAP (South African Police), 57,66,67
SASO (South African Students Organization),
   118
Savimbi, Dr Jonas, 43
Sebe, Chief Lennox, 123
Seme, Dr Pixley, 105,107,108
Sibeko, David, 113
Sisulu, Walter, 21,106,110
Slabbert, Dr Frederick Van Zyl, 34,35,36
Slovo, Joe, 21,118
Smith, David, 49
Smith, Ian, 40,46
Smuts, General Jan, 10,11,12,15,39,104
Sobukwe, Robert, 107,111,113
Soviet Union, 43,47,50,51,52,53,56,57,82,
   109,114,130,131
Strijdom, J.G., 19
Suzman, Helen, 34
SWAPO (South-West Africa People's
   Organization), 27,37,46,51,52,55,56,57,67

T

Tambo, Oliver, 21,106,107,114,121,123
Thatcher, Margaret, 38,97
Theron Commission, 23
Tomlinson Report, 18,19,22

Transkei, 18,21,123
Treurnicht, Dr Andries, 30
TUCSA (Trade Union Congress of South
    Africa), 102
Tutu, Archbishop Desmond, 104,126

U
UCOR (Uranium Corporation of South
    Africa), 84
UDF (United Democratic Front), 104,120,
    121,122,123,126,127,128,129
Umkhonto We Sizwe (*see also* MK), 110,115,
    117
UNITA (National Union for the Total
    Independence of Angola), 41,43,44,51,52,
    67,68,70,91
United Party, 15,16,30,34
UWUSA (United Workers Union of South
    Africa), 103

V
van den Bergh, General H.J., 14,22,26,42,
    43,44
van Rensberg, J.F., 14
Verwoerd, Dr H.J., 5,15,18,19,20,21,40,74,
    79

Villiers, Dr W. de, 85
Vorster, B.J., 1,14,21,22,23,24,25,47,76,96

W
Walls, General Peter, 49,50
Wassenaar, Dr A.D., 99
Wiehahn Commission, 101,102,128
Worrall, Dr Denis, 36,38,72

X
Xuma, Dr Albert, 105,108

Z
ZANLA (Zimbabwean African National
    Liberation Army), 45,48,49,50
ZANU (Zimbabwean African National
    Union), 48
ZANU (PF), 45,48,50,88,116
ZAPU (Zimbabwean African People's
    Union), 48,49
Zimbabwe, 69,87,92,93
ZIPRA (Independent People's Revolutionary
    Army of Zimbabwe), 48,49